LINDA HART-HEWINS / JAN WELLS

# Better Books!
# Better Readers!

*How to choose, use and level books for children in the primary grades*

Stenhouse Publishers

YORK, MAINE

Pembroke Publishers Limited

MARKHAM, ONTARIO

©1999   Pembroke Publishers
538 Hood Road
Markham, Ontario, Canada L3R 3K9
1-800-997-9807

Published in the United States by Stenhouse Publishers
P.O. Box 360
York, Maine 03909
ISBN 1-57110-305-8
www.stenhouse.com

**Canadian Cataloguing in Publication Data**

Hart-Hewins, Linda
   Better books! Better readers!: how to choose, use and level books for
children in the primary grades

Includes bibliographical references.
ISBN 1-55138-105-2

1. Reading (Primary).   2. Children – Books and reading.   I. Wells, Jan,
1948-   .  II. Title.

LB1525.H26  1999      372.4      C98-932986-0

Editor:                    Cynthia Young
Cover Design:              John Zehethofer
Cover Photography:  Ajay Photographics
Typesetting:               Jay Tee Graphics Ltd.
Cover photo taken in Jane Murphy's class at Wells Street Public School.

Printed and bound in Canada
9 8 7 6 5 4 3 2 1

# Table of Contents

# Foreword

I have always centred my own work with children around the best books I could find, powerful resources that grabbed the children intellectually and emotionally. What a pleasure to work with Jan Wells and Linda Hart-Hewins over the years, for from the start, their reading and writing curriculum featured books at the very heart of learning. From their *Borrow a Book* program to their *Real Books for Reading*, these two educators have demonstrated that real books are the stuff of learning, and that young readers and writers deserve nothing but the best.

Jan Wells and Linda Hart-Hewins have written this book "from the inside out," building on their experiences with children and teachers from the context of their work within real classrooms. During their professional years as teachers, administrators, consultants, and writers, they focused on helping children to become effective independent readers, and supporting teachers in creating programs and environments that promote life-long literacy.

Beginning with helpful suggestions for books for beginning, developing, and independent readers, Jan and Linda then offer practical and useful strategies for working alongside those young readers. They encourage new readers to explore text to the fullest, and make as much meaning as possible through talking about what they have read, finding delight and satisfaction in the story, and becoming strong wordsmiths as they manipulate and play with the linguistic bits and pieces of words that matter.

For Jan and Linda, reading and writing are natural and reciprocal components of a successful literacy program. Their anecdotes and descriptions of children and teachers at work paint a picture of education at its best — teachers and children learning together, using all the pieces of print to construct meaning in their lives. These two teachers know how to motivate children into mining a story using books that work, causing the youngsters to dig deep in their quest for understanding, to relate one story to another, to use sets of books to connect ideas, to care about the tales and the tellers, to feel comfortable around print structures, and to develop a love of words and how they work.

For me, learning to be a better teacher starts in the classroom, and Jan and Linda know what it's like to live among the children. They are true educators, always adapting and adding to their knowledge base about how we can help children to become stronger readers and writers. Their ten essential ingredients for a successful language program are comprehensive and, what's more, achievable. You can build a better classroom with this book, and the children you teach will be grateful.

David Booth
Coordinator, Elementary Programs
O.I.S.E.-U. of T.

## Introduction

"Reading like learning to swim takes hours of practice, but the practice must be in a real book that gives as much personal satisfaction as plunging in the cold water of a lake gives to the swimmer."

*Charlotte Huck*

This book is the result of a collaboration over a number of years in which we put into practice our growing conviction that children need real books and real writing experiences to become fluent and enthusiastic readers. We have created a language program which focuses not on the print but on stories; a program in which it is what you can *do* with language that matters. By discovering stories and writers, we have learned something of the power of the written word and its potential for enhancing learning; through the use of real books in our classrooms, we have helped children to become not only literate but also lovers of reading. In Grade 2 David wrote in his reading journal, "Miss Rumphius is my most favorite book of all the books in our collection because she wants to make the world a more beautiful place." He understood not only how to read but also *why* we read. It is a pleasurable thing to do. Through reading we enter another world, the literate world in which experience is mediated through the written word.

### Note

We refer to our classrooms throughout this book. Linda's class was a family-grouped class of kindergarten and Grade 1 students. Jan's class was a family-group of Grade 1 and 2 students.

We have written several books for primary grade teachers who wished to implement literature-based reading and writing programs in their classrooms. We have come to believe that administrators and parents would also find it helpful to understand more about the way that young children are being taught to read in kindergartens and the first three grades. The program we implemented and continue to recommend provides practical guidelines for organizing a classroom to foster the growth of reading and writing in an atmosphere that values play, hands-on activities, and the arts. Our program respects the child's need for ownership and for time to complete self-chosen tasks.

Now, almost a decade since we began our own literature-based program, we are still passionately committed to the use of real books to help children become enthusiastic readers and writers. Through conversations with other educators and parents, we learned that there are many people who agree with us. We see teachers everywhere implementing literature-based reading and writing programs which use real books. However, during these conversations, we found that teachers would like detailed help in grouping or levelling the books they have in their classrooms; in determining the features that make one book harder or easier than another; and in selecting books that offer success rather than frustration to beginning readers.

Teachers want to understand the criteria for placing a book in a given category. What should they be looking for when deciding the category in which a book belongs? And what makes a book suitable for readers with specific skills? Teachers need to sort their own collection of books and incorporate new books quickly into these collections. Thus, in this book, we have outlined our specific criteria for evaluating books. We have identified benchmark books at each level to make it easier for teachers to categorize their own books. These benchmark books are the ones that we have found to be the most reliable with readers at a particular level. For this reason, the benchmark books are also useful for assessment purposes. Our bibliography of books for primary classrooms is a lively and varied selection of titles ranging from favorite old classics by well-known authors to engaging new books by contemporary children's writers.

Reading development progresses in stages. We have identified three broad stages of reading development in this book: Beginning Readers and Writers, Developing Readers and Writers, and Fluent Independent Readers and Writers. For each level of reading development we have identified several categories of books suitable for those readers. Each category is a little harder and more complex than the previous category. However, we have avoided creating too many levels, recognizing from our experience that a very detailed and scientific delineation between levels is unnecessary for regular classroom uses. Keeping the process simple and manageable is important. Too many levels complicate things for us unnecessarily. The three categories we use are discrete enough to be an effective progression, yet broad enough to allow for the reality of managing a classroom program.

Shared Reading and Writing Activities and Guided Reading are two sections we have included in response to the many teachers who asked us for help with specific strategies for working with groups of children.

Shared Reading and Writing and Guided Reading can take place with individual children, and while we feel that individualized instruction is more powerful, we recognize that in reality most teachers need to organize their time so they can work with small groups of children whose needs are similar. These two sections discuss the dynamics of forming groups and suggest teaching strategies for small group work.

Using real books in a literature-based language program involves children working individually, with partners, in small groups, and in the whole-class setting. We focus on activities from which we expect specific learning about reading and writing to emerge. All of these activities involve teaching and learning about stories and writers. Very few of them involve teaching about parts of words or components of sentences. Real books provide real contexts. The activities in our language program keep words, and reading and writing within the meaningful context of each activity.

The chapters that follow describe ten essential ingredients for implementing a successful language program. These ten ingredients are briefly summarized below.

## 1. There Are Real Books in the Classroom
The classroom contains a wide variety of reading materials at the heart of which is a collection of stories and nonfiction materials from which the children choose. This collection is kept fresh by borrowing from the Library Resource Centre and by replacing worn out books. Children also have frequent access to the larger collection in the Library Resource Centre. The bibliography in this book offers teachers a starting point for selecting books for primary classrooms. The same books are used in a wide variety of contexts (read aloud; individual and partner reading; home borrowing; buddy reading; reading to the teacher; and guided and shared reading lessons).

## 2. The Teacher Shares Books With Individuals
The teacher shares books with individual children on a regular basis, encouraging them in their efforts and helping them to develop strategies to unlock the author's meaning; helping them in their choices of books; and discussing their responses and ideas. The teacher keeps anecdotal records in the child's reading log as a routine part of these reading times.

### 3. The Teacher Regularly Holds Guided Reading Sessions With Small Groups of Readers at Similar Levels of Reading Development

In Guided Reading Sessions the teacher uses a set of books that are at the right level for the children in the group. The text stretches their ability without causing frustration. Guided Reading Sessions are used to teach strategies for reading, provide time for guided practice, and offer an opportunity for assessment. The Guided Reading lesson can be a springboard into other literacy activities associated with the book such as story mapping, character portraits, research booklets, and response journals.

### 4. The Teacher Reads Aloud Every Day

Stories are read aloud by the teacher to the class. Sometimes, but not every time, discussion follows and suggestions for possible projects which are related to that story are exchanged. Sometimes a story reading becomes a joint activity, especially if a big book or poetry on a chart is used.

### 5. The Teacher Regularly Holds Whole-Group and Small-Group Shared Reading and Shared Writing Sessions

In Shared Reading the children work together as a group with the teacher to read in unison from a large-size text such as a big book or a chart. In Shared Writing they construct text together, with the teacher scribing on a chart and thinking aloud about which letters and punctuation are needed and how the letters are formed. Shared reading and writing lessons may involve the children in collaborative activities before the text is encountered such as predicting from pictures or looking at artifacts that offer clues as to the content of the story. Strategies such as these encourage prediction and the development of prior knowledge.

### 6. Children Have Time to Practise Reading, Alone or With Another Person

The children read by themselves and to other children from self-selected books made freely available in a comfortable setting. They record their reading in their reading log. For very young children this can be recorded by an adult or they can draw a picture. This log becomes an accumulative record of books enjoyed at school. In some classrooms, parents and younger siblings are invited into the classroom first thing in the morning, and a session of "Noisy Reading" is held with children reading to an adult. Other teachers invite parent volunteers to come into the classroom and listen to children practise their reading.

**7. Children Regularly Borrow Reading Materials to Share at Home**
The children borrow books from the Library Resource Centre and from the classroom to take home. Parents are encouraged to share home reading experiences with their children and invited to make a comment about the book on a special card or in a record book. First-language books and books on tape are always included. In some instances, simple games or books made by the children are included as part of a language homework kit.

**8. Children Regularly Listen to Stories and Read to a Buddy**
This time takes many forms and is dependent upon the needs of the children, the skill of the readers, and the time available. In some instances, the children hear stories read aloud to them by other students and adults within the school. They engage in discussion about those reading experiences and note their responses in a record book or on a comment card. Other times, the children read to their buddies, practising a favorite story. At other times, the children may play a related game, e.g., Snakes and Ladders or Bingo, using the sight vocabulary from a familiar book. In some classrooms, the buddies use their time together to write stories, including making their own versions of a favorite book.

**9. Children Have Time to Write**
The children write daily with a pencil or on a computer about topics of their own choosing. Story making may be inspired by and modelled on the texts shared in the reading program. Writing also takes place in play situations in the classroom.

**10. Reading and Writing Are Part of All Learning**
Children engage in activities that expand the meaning of the stories they have shared. They may retell them, tape-record their own versions, sing, dance, act them out, or represent them by making puppets, constructions of various types, paintings, or drawings. They read and

write as a part of every activity in which they are engaged — reading signs and instructions, writing labels and notices. They are encouraged to notice ways in which reading and writing are used in the real world and to include them in their play whenever possible. Whenever topics or themes of interest are pursued in the classroom, stories and poems that relate to the theme are shared. Collections of thematically linked books are placed in a theme centre. Ideas for special activities suggested by these books are discussed. Themes often start with reading a book, and activities are brainstormed and developed afterward by the children. Whenever children have interests or ideas that they wish to pursue, there is a book or a story to be found that relates to the situation.

These then are the ten components of the program. Before we begin our exploration of these in depth, we will first review the reasons *why* we teach this way, and relate our practice to theory and experience.

ONE 🙿

# *"Reading Takes You Places"*

## The Rationale for a Literature-Rich Reading Program

In the past ten years many primary teachers have moved away from programmed, lock-step reading schemes, which treated all learners like empty vessels waiting to be filled, recognizing that all learners are not the same. Children have different rates of development, different life experiences, different individual tastes and predilections, different learning styles, and, most of all, independent and unique ways of solving problems. In many classrooms the "one-size-fits-all" style of teaching reading was being replaced by methods and materials which acknowledged the diversity of learners in the classroom.

As individualized and literature-based reading made an impact on the lives of children and teachers, the publishing industry kept pace with the change. Many exciting new reading series have been produced in the last ten years, offering a broad range of material for emergent and early readers. In this book we will argue for the use of real (or trade books) in the classroom, as well as the best of the currently available reading series. We will look at different ways of using all sorts of books to bring children to reading. Different sorts of books require different contexts, some being most suitable for reading aloud, some for use in guided reading lessons, and some for shared reading with the whole class. Some books offer the emergent reader essential practice with a known and manageable text that can foster early success. Some books are so compelling that the young reader struggles to read them even though they are beyond the reader's ability. In creating many contexts for reading, the teacher also makes informed judgments about which books to use in a particular context. By offering a wide variety of texts, the teacher offers the child a selection from which they may draw to meet their personal needs. In choosing books for individual or group guided reading, teachers choose books that will allow for guided instruction. When practising reading, children need to encounter text which helps them build their problem-solving strategies. When a child chooses a book the motivation is different. They will look at the pictures and the story or at the information in the book and decide whether or not it interests them. The matching of children's choices with teachers' choices is part of creating a balanced program where there is a place for both.

## *Key Principles*
Our approach to teaching reading is based on several key principles.

- Learning to read is a social and interactive process. It is a quest for meaning, which engages memory and which is embedded in the cultural experience of the reader. The teacher's role is to respect the learning that the child brings to the classroom and to build upon it.
- Reading involves the reader as an active participant. It is the constant struggle to create understanding from the understandings of others. The teacher's role is to create contexts that are meaningful and that actively involve the child as a learner.
- Reading involves a complex combination of cognitive activities that interact in harmony to create meaning. Children learning to read use their oral language experience, their intuitive knowledge of the grammatical system, their common sense or pragmatic view of the world and their knowledge of the alphabetic system to predict word meanings. Learning to read involves learning about letters and the sounds they represent. The teacher's role in helping children learn to read is that of a mediator who builds bridges for the child between the print, and their developing ability to apply their problem solving strategies.
- Learning to read is often a natural and an easy process when chil-

dren grow up in an environment which encourages and fosters a love of reading. It can also be a painful process, slow to evolve and difficult to master. Teachers know that the motivation to read and the active engagement of the learner is key to success. The teacher's role is to communicate enthusiasm and to model a delight in reading that will be irresistible.

When children are invited to tell you what they think reading is they give a variety of answers of which these are typical.

" Reading is fun," wrote Kimmy. "You get to read good stories."
" Reading helps you learn," wrote Jeff.
" Reading makes you use your imagination," said Rajesh.
" Reading a book is a good way to pass the time," wrote Alison.
" Reading helps you spell better," was Ricky's comment.
And from Jason, " Reading takes you to other worlds."

Reading is an adventure for children because the world of books is often a window to the wider world outside their own experience. Through reading they learn about other people and other places; they uncover the secrets of science and technology, from dinosaurs and insects to elephants and airplanes. They read about created, or fantasy, worlds when they enter the world of the imagination in fairytales and legends. Children read about their own world and validate their experiences by recognizing themselves in books. Childhood experiences are demystified when characters in books go through them, too. Getting a pair of glasses, moving house, having a new baby, wanting a puppy — these are everyday experiences that can be hard to deal with. Books help children to make sense of their own lives.

The desire to learn to read is very strong. Books are very attractive objects, colourful and enticing. Young children want access to the mysteries of print and they seek out ways to become literate. Children exposed to books become more and more curious about the words. Children who have contact with adults who mediate the process of reading become hooked on books and are motivated to become independent readers.

## How Do Children Learn Language?

The suggestions we offer in this book are deeply-rooted in some fundamental beliefs about how children learn and how they learn language, in particular. The foundation of our reading and writing program is our belief in these key principles of language learning. They inform our practice and provide us with a basis on which to build the contexts for learning. Before we describe how we construct the classroom program, we will consider why we choose the practices we do.

Language learning takes place because the learner is seeking to achieve other goals — goals which need language to be realized. We don't deliberately set out to learn language, either spoken or written; we acquire language in the pursuit of other activities. A child wants to tell someone about something, or ask a question, or demand attention. Language is the means of communication. To begin with, the child's efforts are immature, they understand the function of language, but lack the necessary forms. The more they use language the more competent they become as they receive feedback from other language users.

As we noted earlier, the imperative to learn how to read is strong because children want to learn from books. And in the process of reading to learn, children learn how to read. Beginning readers lack the necessary strategies for combining all the information from the text into an accurate representation of the words on the page. However, they try to understand, often making up the words to match the pictures, telling themselves a story, or reading the captions under the pictures. They create meaning based on what information they have, and as they receive feedback in the form of encouragement, rereading, and positive reinforcement from adults, they gradually move closer to an accurate reading of the text. As with oral language, the function, or purpose, of reading precedes the form.

We want children to learn to love reading, to become life-long readers, and to have access to the world through books. To want to read, they must see the point of it. Motivation to learn is a key factor in their language acquisition. We discover what language can do and then we determine that we will master it. Children must first discover the power of writing so that they will want to read and write for themselves.

Teachers and parents communicate a love of reading to children so that they want to crack the code. One of the most important things a teacher can do in the language program is to demonstrate through their own reading and writing that they value literacy and literature. We do not teach children to read, they teach themselves. We can only motivate, encourage, and guide the learning. Margaret Meek says:

> "To learn to read, children need the attention of one patient adult, or an older child, for long enough to read something that pleases them both. A book, a person, and shared enjoyment: these are the conditions of success."

We have also learned that language learning is a meaning-making process that begins at birth and continues in the world outside the school regardless of the practices of the school. Children become competent users of their first language without any formal teaching. Speaking, listening, reading, and writing are social as well as cognitive events, and they are driven by the child's inherent curiosity and urge to make sense of things. Children seek explanations and connections. They want to do what others around them do, to have the competencies of their older brothers and sisters, of parents and friends. Frank Smith has called the community of users of written language a "literacy club," and it is this club that young children want to join.

In the world outside the school, people use language to get things done. They write notes to each other, exchange letters, compile lists, and read recipes, instructions, and manuals. They read for pleasure: magazines, newspapers, and books. They read signs and advertisements for information. Children are great imitators; they copy the behavior of the adults around them. William at three wrote scribbles on tiny pieces of paper which he gave to his toys as tickets for the bus. Tara watched her father write out cheques at the supermarket; later he found her with the chequebook writing out her own! Even very young children notice signs in the environment. When her family was passing a Mac's Milk store Megan, at two-and-a-half said, " Look, Mummy, there's my M!"

Language users begin with intentions and purposes and use language to realize those intentions. This is the environment in which children learn to be competent users of their first spoken language before they begin school. It is this environment that enables children to learn a great deal about the written code before they ever have a lesson on the subject and to become efficient readers before they ever meet a reading book. Young children learn that print carries meaning, that it makes sense, and that it does something useful. They *expect* language to be meaningful.

This background knowledge about language, which all children possess, is something which teachers can recognize and value, by capitalizing on it and appreciating how much children already know. We can begin where the child is, and foster their own belief in themselves as readers and writers. We do this through offering a range of classroom activities that use reading and writing in genuine ways, which mirror the ways in which literacy is practised in the world outside the classroom. In our view, school learning and home learning should be much more similar. Classrooms should look and feel more like homes. A classroom is our home for six hours a day, and it is a place where a community lives, sharing the ups and downs of daily life. The climate of the classroom is our first consideration, and the nurturing and caring that take place in primary classrooms are fundamental to our practice as teachers of reading. We construct a program that offers children ways to be expert users of reading and writing from the very start.

*Reading and writing must be authentic acts for genuine purposes.*

The following examples show how children use their reading and writing skills for authentic or genuine purposes.

Karl wanted to leave a structure in the building corner so that he could return to it next day. He left these messages.

The writing shows us that Karl knows that notices can both request compliance and give orders. Interestingly, he orders his classmates not to touch but politely requests the caretaker to leave the structure standing. He already has a sense of different audiences.

18

George wrote this letter to his father to tell him how sad he was that he had to go away on business and how much he missed his cuddling!

Dear Daddy,
I missed you.
I'm glad you came home.
I missed your Cuddling.
I was very sad when you had to leve and now I'm very happy you came back
George

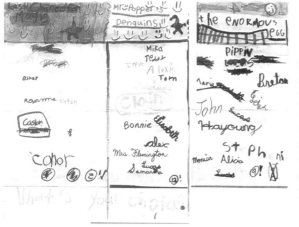

Sasha and Millie completed this survey as part of a reading assignment. They devised the format and surveyed their classmates to see which story was the most popular.

This menu was designed by a group of Grade 2 girls. It is very detailed and groups the selections according to type (e.g., drinks, sandwiches). The authors obviously have considerable experience with menus — the prices are quite accurate. A Sushi Plate can be purchased for $10.50 while a hot dog is only $2.00!

Mira and Jocelyn wrote this explanation of how they got a bulb to light using two wires and a battery.

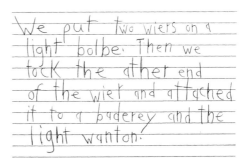

We put two wiers on a light bolbe. Then we tock the other end of the wier and attached it to a baderey and the light wanton.

More and more teachers are asking their students to write explanations of what was done and learned. When students write an explanation like this, they consolidate their learning.

The classroom contexts in which these pieces of writing were generated allowed the children to use written language for their own authentic purposes. For children to see reading and writing as purposeful, it too must arise from a genuinely felt desire. Whether snuggled among the pillows of the reading corner, or shared with the teacher at a table, or undertaken with a friend to find out about something of interest, reading and writing must be purposeful. Children learn to read by reading and they learn to write by writing. The teacher's job involves creating contexts where reading and writing can happen.

## How Do Children Learn to Read?

As a teacher of reading it is important to have a clear idea of what constitutes the act of reading. Its complexity is enormous. The unanswered questions about reading which fuel on-going research can sometimes seem overwhelming. The child who is hard to teach always raises the conundrum, what is the best method? The success of most children regardless of the teaching methods can seem miraculous. As much as we may try to define reading scientifically, it remains elusive, for there is an emotional or affective component in both learning to read and in being a life-long reader that defies analysis.

We try to offer as many ways to success as we can, bearing in mind that some children learn best visually, some are auditory learners, some are kinesthetic learners. Howard Gardner has taught us that there are seven (or perhaps more) "intelligences" or ways of seeing the world. Some people excel in one area, and some, in others. Each person seems to be oriented towards particular ways of learning and representing that learning. As teachers of reading we want to present the information about the world of literacy to students in a wide variety of ways so that each may find a way in. Everything from games, songs, poetry, listening centres, quiet times, sharing books aloud, reading with friends and reading alone, and working with paint, music, modelling and constructing materials — all of these are part of teaching reading. What the child needs to learn is how to use a variety of strategies to understand the meaning of print. Our job is to teach those strategies, to help children use them, and to continue to monitor their use.

Reading and understanding what we read is an interaction between three categories of information, or "cuing systems," that operate simultaneously in a social or situational context. Knowledge of the cuing systems is subconsciously held and used intuitively, but it is fundamental to reading.

### 1. Meaning Cues

The *semantic* cuing system involves the reader's common-sense knowledge of what words mean. What do they refer to in the real world? The use of this information depends upon the reader's schema, that is, their previous experience of the concepts involved. The context in which the words occur is crucial to this understanding. Kenneth Goodman calls the act of reading "a psycholinguistic guessing game" in which the reader makes predictions and confirms these by reference to the text. Thus, when we see a sign on the door of a store we may predict that it will say Entrance or Exit, Open or Closed. If it is only eight o'clock in the morning we probably guess that it says Closed. We apply our common sense knowledge of stores and the way they operate, or our schema for stores. Obviously this has implications for the reading that young children can accomplish independently. If they have no experience of a word and the concept to which it refers, they will find it harder to read that word.

We have noticed repeatedly that beginning readers tackling John Stadler's book *Hooray for Snail* would invariably make the same miscue. Where the text says "Snail slams the ball," they read, "Snail hits the ball," despite the visual information to the contrary. We wondered why this should be and then realized that the semantic cuing system is taking precedence over the grapho-phonic. This is because the story has reached the point where the snail is up to bat. The picture shows him hitting the ball. The word "slams" is not the obvious one for this concept. The semantic cues from the story and the picture, together with the child's schema for bats and balls leads to the miscue nine times out of ten. Children who rely *solely* on phonics often stall at the word "slams," and may have trouble continuing. When teaching strategies for reading, we emphasize to children that what makes sense, or your best guess, is often the best way to crack an unknown word.

### 2. Syntactic Cues

The second cuing system is the *syntactic*, and it depends on the reader's knowledge of the spoken language. Language is rule-governed, and a knowledge of syntax is an understanding of the rules which determine how words are combined to make sense. Subconsciously, all speakers of a language have mastery of the syntax of that language. They know without needing to articulate the knowledge that nouns, verbs, adjectives, adverbs, prepositions, and conjunctions have to be combined in a certain order in a sentence. English speakers do not have to be taught that word order is fundamental to meaning in English. "The boy ate the big peach" makes sense syntactically, but "Boy the ate peach big" does not. As we read, our uncertainty about the text is constantly reduced, as the range of syntactic possibilities in any particular position in a sentence is limited. This has implications for second-language learners, as their control of this cuing system is less automatic than that of a native speaker.

It has been our experience that the small function words in a sentence, words such as *and, the, a, at, but,* and *so*, prove to be the hardest for young children to learn by sight, because there are no concepts on which to hook the words. It is also the case that function words, while they are short and appear frequently in all text, are almost redundant in the reading process. A sentence with function words removed is still readable; the eye hardly needs to see these words. Our knowledge of syntax allows us to fill in the conjunctions and prepositions, definite and indefinite articles. When young children who are reading to us hesitate, we always fill in these little words quickly, because we don't want them to lose the flow of the language and struggle to sound out these words at the expense of meaning. Function words soon become automatic through their constant practice in the children's daily writing. Because they are high-frequency words, they will be spelled over and over again and eventually will be recognized when encountered in reading. The syntactic cuing system becomes noticeable when it is *not* used; when a child guesses a word that does not make sense grammatically. As a means of getting meaning from print, it never operates in isolation from the other two cuing systems — the semantic and the grapho-phonic. There is a constant interaction among all three.

### 3. Visual Cues

The third cuing system is the *grapho-phonic*. Traditionally it has been assumed that children must achieve mastery of phonics to learn how to read. A large amount of time is spent in some classrooms teaching phonic rules. However, there are so many of these rules that no one — not even the most successful and fluent reader, and especially not a beginning reader — could articulate them all. Phonics serves a purpose in reading development. It supports the natural associations children make between letters and sounds when they learn the alphabet. But mastery of phonic rules for the sake of mastery is a sadly misguided application of the strategy.

Knowing the alphabet is part of reading. The letters occuring in the first part of a word are of particluar importance because they are a signal to the reader. The first letter, usually a consonant, triggers the reader to bring together the other cuing systems and to make meaning. In other words, children need to know the alphabet. When they encounter an unknown word they need to look at the pictures, think about the story, ask themselves what would make sense, and use the first letters of the word as a springboard to the meaning. When reading the opening lines of Eric Carle's **The Very Hungry Caterpillar**, "In the light of the moon a little egg lay on a leaf," there are very few children who read "In the light of the sun" even though it makes perfect sense. The letter "M" precludes the word, and as the picture has a face it must be the moon. The semantic and syntactic information is confirmed by the letter cue.

The twenty-six letters of the alphabet are learned in a variety of ways. For many children this learning takes place in the home and the preschool through games like I Spy, through the writing of family names, and the recognition of letters in the environment. The letters of a child's own name are often the first to be learned. In the classroom the alphabet is mastered through daily reading and writing. As children write they are forced to draw upon their alphabetic knowledge to construct words. Daily writing is therefore a key component of our reading program. Through writing the children come to know the sounds the letters make. Other methods of directly teaching the alphabet, through stories, songs, wall displays, games, and puzzles, all contribute to the growing knowledge of sound-symbol correspondence that is essential for fluent reading.

Reading is far more complex than simply knowing letters and sounding them out to form words. It is an act of construction, of building meanings. Constance Weaver has described the interaction between reader and text as "an ever fluctuating dance that occurs more or less simultaneously on and across various levels: letters, words, sentences, schemata; writer, text and reader; text/reader and context; the present reader with other readers, past and present; and so forth; all connected in a multi-dimensional holarchy, an interlocking network or web of meaning, a synchronous dance . . ."

Inevitably we face the dilemma of whether or not we should reject methods that attempt to teach only parts of words and words out of context. We have found that *all three* cuing systems are part of reading, but that any one of them, used for reading words and parts of words outside a meaningful context renders them less useful. Ultimately, we choose to avoid stilted and artificial texts that focus only on parts of words, on words out of context, or on one single strategy for decoding text. This means that we must have a wide range of reading material, fiction and nonfiction, in our classrooms. For if fluent readers use the three cuing systems together in interaction, then it is clearly nonsense to provide text for beginning readers that bars their access to two-thirds of the available information. A child's first reading book must make sense and offer as much contextual and syntactic support as possible.

## What are "Real" Books and Why Do We Use Them?

We believe that the materials presented to young readers are the texts which teach what readers learn and that the construction of these texts is of primary importance. There must be a congruence between our beliefs about how children learn and our selection of books and other materials which foster the learning. For us, the world of children's literature, both fiction and nonfiction, is the starting point for our classroom collection, and this book reflects our belief in the power of books to teach children to read.

Real books, or trade books, published for sale in bookstores or for distribution in libraries, are distinguished from reading series in several ways, but the major difference is simply one of intent. In writing for a reading series an author is purposely meeting the objective of creating material that can be used to teach reading. A children's author, on the other hand, has no such imperative. The writing comes from a desire to communicate with children and to add to the experience of childhood through the creation of stories which delight and please the reader. Some writers, like Eve Bunting, write to change children's perceptions of the world and increase their social awareness. *Fly Away Home* (about a boy and his father who live in Chicago's O'Hare Airport) and *Going Home* (about Mexican migrant workers) are deeply touching stories which open children's eyes to the diversity of the human experience. Some writers, like Tony Ross, Babette Cole, and Robert Munsch are irreverent, challenging stereotypes and turning the world topsy-turvy. *Princess Smartypants* and *Princess Tough* are favorites because they challenge the accepted view of things. Some writers, such as Shirley Hughes, write stories which reflect the day-to-day lives of children and immortalize those moments that mean so much: losing a toy like *Dogger* or getting locked out like Alfie in *Alfie Gets Home First*. Books such as these offer children something to think about.

In families there are often books that are favorites, read aloud frequently, and even memorized word for word. The stories of Beatrix Potter, despite their archaic English and difficult words, are beloved by many young children for the rhythms of the language and the power of the storytelling. Most adults can remember one or two favorites from childhood: *Mike Mulligan and his Steamshovel*; *The Story of Ferdinand*; *The Velveteen Rabbit*. Sometimes catch-phrases become part of a family's shared memory. In our house we loved the story by Janet and Allan Ahlberg called *Burglar Bill*. As Burglar Bill goes about his business (before he meets Burglar Betty and the baby and reforms his ways), he breaks into houses and steals. "That's a nice umbrella," he says. "I'll have that. That's a nice tin of beans. I'll have that." And so on. It has been years since we read *Burglar Bill*, but when out shopping in a big department store, it is not unusual for one of us to murmur, "That's a nice sweater. I'll have that." The language of a good story somehow enters the imagination and becomes part of the reader. We take it and make it ours, savoring it, enjoying the joke, sharing it amongst ourselves, and bringing it out to trigger happy memories. It is this language that is created by writers that can only be found in real books. These are the books that are at the heart of our classroom program. These books are found in school and public libraries, and reading them is part of growing up literate in our culture.

The myriad of "little books," which are available from all the major publishers, and which we list in our bibliography, are excellent books for beginning readers to use for practice. They offer ways of ensuring success in the early stages of reading development. They offer the teacher sets of texts which are suitable for guided reading lessons and practice in small groups. These books go hand in hand with the works of children's authors and the trade books which are not part of a reading series.

Books for practising reading in the early stages may be trade books or from packaged series, but they must have certain characteristics if they are to offer the maximum support to the early reader. The language must be predictable both semantically and syntactically. Look again at the opening lines of Eric Carle's *The Very Hungry Caterpillar*:

> "In the light of the moon a little egg lay on a leaf. One Sunday morning the warm sun came up and — pop! — out of the egg came a very small and very hungry caterpillar. He started to look for some food."

The picture of the moon, the egg, and the leaf provide a context in which to set the story and so assist the child's attempt to read the words. The logic of the story also provides an internal context. What comes out of eggs on leaves? And what else would a hungry caterpillar do except start to look for food? We find that most children can read the story of *The Very Hungry Caterpillar* with very little practice. The text itself teaches them, and the story as it unfolds provides the motivation to read. The rhythm of the language supports the reader and offers confirmation of expectations. The days of the week follow one after the other; numbers increase in order from one to five as the pages turn; and after each feed, the caterpillar. . . "was still hungry!" The pictures fill the pages with light and color. Real holes are made as the caterpillar "chews" his way through the book, and they appeal to the curiosity and sense of discovery of the children, who turn the pages eagerly to find him emerging from the fruits. There is no need to teach them to turn the pages in order. Finally, children can identify with the caterpillar's encounter with too many rich foods, leading to: "That night he had a stomach ache."

The experience of reading this book is a *literary* experience as well as an act of reading. It is worth doing for its own sake and there is an ultimate satisfaction in it. The books we use in school should be like the best of books that children read at home, and the interactions that they have with books in school should also mirror the genuine acts of reading that take place outside the school. The language activities that go on in classrooms should involve finding information, using instructions, writing messages, keeping records and recording observations, making lists and reading them, sharing reactions to stories, and creating our own stories to share with others.

The sort of storybooks that are shared at home and loved by children and parents alike are the sort of books that should be available in classrooms. The sort of stories that are to be found at the public library are the sort of stories that should be found in school. The things that are done with those books should closely mirror the genuine purposes for which books are intended. Books give pleasure and knowledge. The communal reading of them brings members of families into contact and builds a store of shared experience. Some of the patterns and memories of family life revolve around the times when adults read to children.

There is another argument, perhaps the most important, for using real books in the early reading program. We use real books because we want to foster a love of reading. Unless they want to read, children won't read. Unless they gain satisfaction and joy from the act of reading, they will see it as a chore. If it is a chore they will not become life-long readers. Literature is not simply a means of entertaining and amusing children. It is essential nourishment for their imaginations, their hearts, and their minds. It contributes to their personal growth by widening their horizons, giving them experiences of people and places out of time and out of space; long ago and far away; or here and now, but different from themselves. It gives them experiences of personal confirmation when the child in the book is a child with thoughts and fears, adventures and misadventures like their own. It gives them experiences of profound emotional and psychological power. It helps them make sense of their own experience and the experiences of others. People who enjoy reading may not be better human beings, but they are aware that they have access to a range of feelings and experiences that would not otherwise be available to them. When questioned, most adult readers acknowledge that they came to the love of reading during childhood.

Literature which has integrity explores the human experience. It orders and evaluates it, illuminates its heights and depths, and gives us images to think with and metaphors for living. Children who do not come to a love of reading miss this essentially humanizing experience. Michele Landsberg writes:

"The adult who takes the time to learn something of children's books and to pass them on with enthusiasm and care gives something precious to the child — and gives something priceless to the world: a child deep rooted in language and story, a child with an educated heart."

Paul Hazard put it metaphorically:

"Give us books, say the children, give us wings."

Finally, we use literature in the reading program because it works. We see children becoming successful readers and learning much more than a system for decoding the basal reader for that grade. We hear children talking about their favorite authors or the way that a story can make you feel creepy or sad. They talk about the way that it's not fair that E.B. White never tells you what happened to Margoles in the story of **Stuart Little**, and that **John Brown, Rose and the Midnight Cat** is about being jealous, "like when you have a new baby." We hear them recommend books to each other. We see them learn to discriminate between books that leave you wondering, like those of Chris Van Allsberg and Maurice Sendak, and those that leave nothing to their imagination. They develop favorites and return to the same book again and again.

Children who learn to read with real books begin to think like writers. They see the structure of stories and borrow these for their own story writing. They find vocabulary in their reading that enriches their writing. They learn how to describe characters and places in a story and how to talk about what is significant in a plot. They learn how to present factual information, how to write captions for pictures, and how to inform their readers of the main idea. The books they read provide models for structure and style. Reading and writing are learned hand in hand, the one enriching the other. We cannot teach writing without providing the best possible examples of how to write.

And so we fill our classroom with books. In the next chapter we will look at book selection. Which books do we choose and for which purposes? What is good literature for children, and how do we help students find the right book at the right time? How do we organize and level the books so that they can be accessed easily for different purposes?

Children learning to read need to be able to choose from a wide range of material. The teacher mediates between the child and the print, teaching strategies for understanding, and helping scaffold the child's developing expertise. Children must be offered the opportunity to find the books that suit their needs, their personality, their interests, and their learning style. The classroom becomes a place where adventure and imagination are fuelled by literature; where children's writing is inspired by the writers they read; and where ideas — the currency of learning — are found in many places, including the pages of books.

TWO 🙷

# Stocking Your Classroom Library

C.S. Lewis wrote,

> "No book is really worth reading at the age of ten which is not equally (and often far more ) worth reading at the age of fifty."

## Books and Children: Finding the Right Fit

We might argue that a good book for a five-year-old also has a timeless appeal which means that both adults and children can enjoy it. What makes a good book for children? How can we select books for our classrooms that will meet the various needs of our young readers? When we open our classrooms to the world of children's books, how can we know that the books will be appropriate for the age of the children and their stage of reading development?

**We need to seek a quality and an integrity in the writing and the illustrations which are lasting.** This is why series books, written by a computer, can never be more than transitory experiences. Children outgrow them because they offer little of substance. There is no writer to communicate with them. One of the first questions that a teacher should ask when choosing books for the classroom is "Do I like this book and will I enjoy reading this with children?"

I remember a Grade 8 student who told me that when she was little she had hated the monsters in *Where the Wild Things Are.* After a session in which we had been responding to picture books and discovering some of the many motifs in that book, she said that she now saw it differently. She was intrigued by Sendak's exploration of the boy's subconscious mind. She thought that the pictures had probably scared her as a child because she had fears which she couldn't identify but which might be manifest as monsters. Books such as this one have many layers, which we peel away like the skin of an onion to reach the significance of the book for us. Each time we return to it at a different stage in life, we see new meanings.

Often adults respond to a stratum of meaning which is not recognized by the young children who enjoy the book for other reasons. *Peepo!* by Janet and Allan Ahlberg is full of visual treats for child readers as they follow the day of a baby and see the world through his eyes. For the adult reader, the nostalgic illustrations are evocative of times gone by; wartime Britain is the setting for the story. And the everyday happenings of the family emphasize the continuity of family life and some of its humor. Robert Munsch, speaking of his stories *The Paper Bag Princess* and *Love you Forever*, has called this dual appeal "bi-modality." In the best children's books there is a little something for the adult reader to appreciate.

When selecting books for children, however, we must take care that adult tastes do not predominate. Children often love to read material about which we may feel less than enthusiastic. There may be some books that we can't stand, but which the children really enjoy. We must be careful of being critical of the books children choose. We must learn to find what it is in those books that appeals to them so that we may guide their reading toward other books that will also satisfy but perhaps be more challenging in the ideas they present. If children are to engage in the reading process, they must find the experience both enjoyable and relevant. Otherwise, their participation will be only superficial and temporary.

Conversely, we must not expect children to enjoy books just because we do. Many picture books now available are written for increasingly sophisticated audiences. Both illustrations and subject matter found in such books as Paul Yee's *Ghost Train* are aimed at a mature audience and are best used in later grades. If you find yourself reading a book that is too sophisticated for young children, they will let you know. When you start to lose your audience it is a sure sign that the story is not holding their attention. Learning how to abandon a book is one of the reading skills we want to foster. Asking the class, "What do you think so far?" will often lead to honest responses that will suggest that you abandon a story. Be straightforward with the class. Sometimes we say, " Really, I'm not enjoying reading this to you. Do you mind if I stop?"

## A CLEAN *Approach*

We believe there are five major points to consider when selecting books for a primary classroom program. These are the criteria that we take into account when selecting books for the classroom.

1. **Content**: What is the book about? Who is depicted and how?
2. **Language**: How is the content expressed?
3. **Ease of reading:** What is the difficulty and legibility of the text?
4. **Attractiveness:** Does this book look and feel attractive?
5. **Need:** Does this material broaden and deepen the collection?

### 1. Content

Young children have a fundamental need to hear the world represented in story. In fact it is a right of childhood, a developmental necessity. Our collection of books will be first and foremost a collection of stories: traditional tales, folk and fairy stories, legends, myths, and wonder tales. It will include stories written by contemporary authors who use traditional formulas, repetition, and accumulation: writers such as Robert Munsch, Pat Hutchins, Phoebe Gillman, Mem Fox, and Eric Carle.

Teachers now include nonfiction materials in the collection because most children are fascinated by the world around them. From a very early age, they have many questions to be answered. Books about mammals, sea creatures, cars, trucks, and the universe appeal to girls as well as boys. In recent years there has been a profusion of simple, easy-to-read nonfiction materials. Books such as the *Eye Spy Series* and *Wonder Works* provide many hours of enjoyment for beginning readers.

Children also love the sound of poetry and rhyme, and there is strong evidence that hearing poetry develops phonemic awareness in young children. Books such as *One, Two, Buckle My Shoe* and *Crackers and Crumbs* help to broaden and deepen the appeal of the collection. Adding poetry to the collection helps us to develop an eclectic mix that offers a reason for all of the children to listen and to read.

It is important that the books are relevant to the children who read them; that they reflect a world familiar to the child; and that they deal with ideas and experiences at an age-appropriate level. Books provide a safe framework in which children can explore some of their psychological needs. All of us inevitably face change, trouble, loss, and uncertainty. These and many other emotional issues may be confronted and dealt with in books. One of the most important functions of literature for children is to reassure them that they are not alone in feeling as they do. Such concepts may be part of stories which have fantasy settings. *Peter Rabbit*, for example, is the archetypal naughty boy who must suffer the consequences of his disobedience, while his good little brothers and sisters eat bread, milk, and blackberries. *Curious George* is another favorite. The naughty monkey who is too inquisitive has delighted children for generations. In Jan's class the children began to call anyone who asked a lot of questions "Curious George"!

Other books show contemporary settings and children of all races and colors engaged in everyday activities. Ezra Jack Keats was one of the first artists and writers to show us black children in urban settings. *The Snowy Day* is a classic picture book, about a small boy's pleasure in the snow, to which most children can relate. It is important to provide a balance between the real and the imaginary, the urban and the rural, the past and the present. Our children need to see themselves as they are, as well as in metaphors. Gary was a Nigerian boy newly arrived in our community. His face lit up with smiles when Jan read Jan Ormerod's *Eat Up, Gemma*. The brother who solves Gemma's eating problem looked exactly like Gary. Children need to see themselves in the stories they read.

The content of children's books must be free from racial and sexual stereotyping and bias. Overt racism and sexism is often easy to spot. It is less obvious when it is implied by exclusions or by omission; for example, when books depict characters only in certain roles. Not too long ago it was impossible to find a father who cooked, or a mother who went to the office in a children's book. It is now possible to build a collection which contains stories and illustrations which show all people behaving in positive ways and in urban twentieth-century settings. *Red Parka Mary*, *Grace and Family*, and *K is for Kiss* are excellent examples of books that have a compelling story and that accurately depict children of many races and religions in everyday situations.

When there are bilingual children in the class, many teachers seek out books in the children's first language or look for dual-text editions. There are bilingual books which are translations of familiar English stories such as *Badger's Parting Gifts* and *Where's Spot?* There are also traditional stories from other cultures such as *Mouse Bride* and *The Rainbow Fish.* There is a growing presence of first-language materials, but it may still be necessary for teachers to enlist the help of bilingual parents or staff in creating dual text editions of favorite books. Teachers show respect for the cultural background of the children they teach by the presence of these books in their classrooms. They also make it possible for the families of their children to share books at home more easily.

### 2. Language

The language of the book is important in three ways. First, it is through the words of the text that children come to experience "writerly" ways of expression. Margaret Meek writes that: "The most important single lesson that children learn from texts is the nature and variety of written discourse, the different ways that language lets a writer tell, and the many and different ways a reader reads."

Consider again the opening sentence of *The Very Hungry Caterpillar:* "In the light of the moon a little egg lay on a leaf." Most people would *tell* that information in a different way. The writer shines new light on an ordinary event. He fills a simple description with possibilities. The language of storytellers is filled with rhythm and rhyme, metaphor and simile. Our first encounters with these forms of written language is in the literature that is used in children's books. The richness of words should never be diminished by attempts to simplify text for beginning readers.

Secondly, the language of the text is important because it introduces new vocabulary to children and links those words to concepts that may be outside of the child's actual experience. This way, their knowledge of the world and the words that refer to that knowledge is increased and their vocabulary grows. During a visit to the Caribbean,

Anthony saw panniers on a donkey and said, "Oh, that's real. I thought it was only in books." Children's views of reality and fantasy are shaped by the stories they are read and told. Young children are still sorting out whether or not there really are slippers made of glass, carpets that fly, and donkeys that carry panniers. The more books children read, the more they come to know.

Thirdly, language can help or hinder fledgling readers in their efforts to make sense of text. The collection must include many easy-to-read texts with simple, repetitive structures that support the efforts of the children in developing strategies for independence. Some of these books may be home-made, written by the children themselves, using key words from their own vocabulary. Some may be made by teachers, using the experiences of the class as their subject matter. Simple, familiar, and easily memorized, these books are a starting point for all young children as they move into literacy.

### 3. Ease of Reading

The classroom collection needs to provide a range of books that meets the many different skill levels of the readers. For independent practice, guided reading, and teacher conferences, the children need books that are at their independent and their instructional levels. Teachers must provide variety within each level to allow the children to find something that is of interest. How can we determine readability levels and ensure that we have sufficient material that is easy enough to read? Trade books are designed and printed in a wide variety of sizes, shapes, fonts, and formats. The ease or difficulty of a book for a child reader derives from the complex interaction between several factors. When creating a classroom collection which is organized by levels, teachers must consider the language and textual features that contribute to readability:

- size of print;
- number of pages;
- number of words on a page;
- number of words in a sentence;
- where line breaks occur (at the end of a clause makes for easier reading);
- the match between the words and the pictures (is the meaning obvious?);

- language patterns, i.e., syntactic predictability;
- repetition of sentences;
- repetition of refrains;
- rhyming words;
- words from children's oral language;
- words that repeat frequently;
- words and sentences that are predictable from pictures;
- story structures that drive the reader to the conclusion; and
- stories that are personally relevant to the reader.

**Size of Print**

The larger the print, the easier it is for the young reader to see the configurations of the words. *Four Black Puppies* is a good example of a "First Steps" book that has large, clear print that easily matches the illustrations. However, *Coco Can't Wait*, a book with a good match between the illustrations and the text and only a small amount of print on each page, is much harder to read because the print is very small. Books in the first three levels of our bibliography all have large, clear print.

**Number of Words on a Page**

Initially, children often read familiar words from the everyday environment — traffic signs, the names of local supermarkets, restaurants, and the names of their family members. They read familiar single words. Concept books with one word on the page, such as the *Baby's Catalogue* and simple alphabet books, offer instant success for the fledgling reader. Too many words on a page often confuse and overwhelm young children. As the amount of text on the page increases so must the stamina and skill of the reader. Predictably then, developing readers find the *Frog and Toad* books much harder to read than *Gone Fishing* and *My Tooth is Loose*. All of these books use language that resembles oral language patterns, have good matches between the illustrations and the text, and have reasonably large, clear print. What makes the one book harder than another is primarily the *amount* of print on a page.

**The Number of Words in a Sentence**

Another factor to be considered when deciding the level of readability of a particular book is the number of words in a sentence. Compound and complex sentences that contain a number of words and clauses require more skill from the reader than text that relies on simple short sentences. Thus, readers find text from books such as *The Ugly Duckling* and *Old Bag of Bones: A Coyote Tale* easier to read than Jane Kurtz' *Fire on the Mountain*, or *The Boy Who Lived With the Seals* by Rafe Martin.

### Where the Line Break Occurs

Beginning readers get easily confused by too many words on a page and sentences that are too long and complex. Initially they seem to have difficulty remembering ideas from one line to another and from one page to another. They get lost easily and often need us to re-read the text and help them reposition themselves. For our very earliest readers we carefully select material in which the line and page breaks are at the end of a clause or a sentence. Print that is broken mid-line or between pages makes the material harder to read. Thus, children often find "First Novels" such as *Grandpa Chatterji* or *Sadako and the Thousand Paper Cranes* harder to read than picture books such as *Mrs. Katz and Tush* by Patricia Polacco, or *Wolf Island*, by Celia Godkin because the text in the First Novels carries over from page to page.

### The Match Between the Words and the Pictures

The quality of the illustrations in books for young children plays a critical role in helping to determine the ease with which a beginning reader can find success. The illustrations in a book help readers to set the context for the text. They help to narrow down the choices of what the words might say. The better the match between the illustrations and the text the easier it is for readers to make accurate predictions. Books such as *Four Black Puppies* and *Just Like Daddy* have a good match. The pictures accurately cue the reader to the story line. In order to determine the effectiveness of the match we like to cover up the text and try to tell the story from the pictures. Some books such as *The Bear and the Picnic* by Sarah Hayes appear to have a good match. However, when we covered up the words we found that the illustrations did not give good clues. This helped us to understand why this book seemed harder for the beginning reader than we expected.

**The Format Used in the Book**

Format refers to the design features of the book such as font, page lay-out, size, and shape. Many books use interesting illustrations and have special features. Pop-up books are enormously popular. As young readers eagerly look for what is under the next flap, they naturally read from the front to the back of the book, an important skill to be learned. *Peekaboo Baby!* and *The Hokey Pokey* are excellent examples of books where the format of the story drives the reader to the conclu-sion. However, other unusual formats sometimes make the task of reading more difficult. The *Meg and Mog* books, *Round Trip*, and *Mama Don't Allow* are more difficult to read because the text is either scattered over the page, goes around the edge of the page, or contains speech bubbles.

**Language Patterns: Repetitions of Sentences, Phrases, and Words**

Syntactically predictable material forms the foundation of the collec-tion in the early stages. Children, when they first begin to unlock the print for themselves, rely heavily on the patterns of the language. They quickly memorize the patterns and read the stories with enthusiasm. *I Went Walking* and *The Cat on the Mat* are good examples of books that have a strong pattern with only one or two word-changes from page to page. Children also find books such as *My Cat Likes to Hide In Boxes* and *I Know An Old Lady Who Swallowed a Fly* relatively easy to read because the text is cumulative. Each page repeats the text found on the previous pages. Other books are made easier by the repetition of a sin-gle word or phrase. Even though the pictures are quite complicated in *A Dark, Dark Tale* children often have quick success because Ruth Brown has carefully repeated a phrase of the text from one page to the next and included on each page the words "dark, dark." Children love this book, carefully turning the pages to see what will happen next and following the adventures of the little cat as he explores the "dark, dark house."

When we select books we take special care to ensure that we include many books in which the language patterns are predictable. We read the stories *aloud* to see if the text *sounds* right. It is important to have as many books as possible for this early stage, because it is through suc-cess with these predictable books that the children build a bank of known familiar words, and learn to read from left-to-right and from page to page. Sentence patterns that change from page to page place too many demands on these early readers.

### Repetition of Refrains

Stories that have a refrain offer wonderful opportunities for children to join in the reading. Teachers often find that children naturally chime in when stories such as *The Napping House* and *Going on a Lion Hunt* are read. Materials that have a strong refrain are suitable for shared reading activities. They offer the reader a safe way to experience success as the reading is shared. The beginning reader often feels comfortable reading the refrain parts while another more skilled reader reads the rest of the story. Stories enjoyed in Shared Reading are reread independently or borrowed for reading at home. It is this repeated reading which provides practice and gradually develops independence.

### Rhyming Words

We recommend that stories told in rhyme be included when teachers are purchasing books for their collection. These stories are very supportive of young readers and aid predictions. However, be careful in your search for materials that have a rhyme: you don't want to sacrifice the content. Books such as *Each Peach Pear Plum* have a strong storyline as well as rhyme. The Dr. Seuss books are famous examples of stories told in rhyme beloved by generations of children. Rhyme in itself, however, does not make a book easy to read. In deciding where to place a book in the collection, the rhyme is only one factor to consider alongside all the others, such as number of words and size of print.

Books which contain poems for young children are also important. Children seem naturally to play with language. They love to listen to poetry and nursery rhymes. They often make up rhymes of their own and, in doing so, develop an ear for the rhymes and cadences of language. The poems read at Shared Reading time, collected in children's individual poetry books, and displayed around the room offer more opportunities for repeated readings.

### Words from Children's Oral Language

In most instances stories that closely follow oral language patterns are easier for children to read than those that do not. These stories are sometimes called natural language texts and are modelled on children's oral language. Such texts are especially designed to create links between written language and the way children talk, thus creating a bridge to more literary texts. (Clay, 1991 a) Books such as *The Last Puppy* and *Mine's the Best* contain vocabulary and sentence structures with which most young children are familiar. They can relate to the topic and the conversations and so can more easily make accurate predictions about the text. Other books such as *Peepo!* and *Wilfred Gordon McDonald Partridge* use words which are more complex and full of imagery. The rhythms are used less often in everyday speech and are thus less familiar to children. This does not mean, however, that children should only be exposed to stories that contain familiar vocabulary. In fact, quite the contrary is true. They need to hear many stories that are full of rich and imaginative language, for it is by hearing these stories that children eventually read increasingly complicated text for themselves. In deciding how difficult a book is, consider whether the vocabulary is part of the children's everyday language and whether the speech patterns are familiar.

**Books That are Personally Relevant to the Reader**

However well we level our collection there is one more factor that determines whether or not a child will find the book easy or hard, and that is their own motivation. A girl in Linda's Grade 1 class was determined to read *Charlotte's Web* for herself. She persevered, despite the length and complexity of this novel. She read and re-read the book to anyone who would listen. She badgered people to help her with difficult words until she finished the book for herself. Another little boy was fascinated by trucks. His father was a truck driver, so the boy wanted to know more about trucks. He showed very little interest in imaginative stories but spent hours reading simple nonfiction books about transport. His need to learn was one of the keys to his learning to read. The more we work with beginning readers, the more we are convinced that there is no one set of books that will ensure that all children learn. We agree with Brian Cambourne when he says that learners must see the need to learn and must come to accept responsibility for their own learning. That is why it is critical to have a wide range of reading resources available in the classroom from which the children may select materials that are of interest to them.

## 4. Attractiveness

Books for young children are more attractive than ever as a result of changes in printing technology and the large number of artists and writers now working in the picture-book genre. Books for children should be attractive to look at and to handle. There is no need for us to have torn or broken books in our classrooms. Paperback books can be reinforced by covering them with clear plastic, which extends their life span by several years. The budget to replace worn paperbacks can be obtained when we consider these resources as essential and an alternative to workbooks. A classroom rich in literature has no need of dull drills and exercises. The money formerly spent on these can be used to buy better books.

The pictures are an important part of a first reading book, not only because illustrations embellish text, but also because they provide contextual clues that assist the reader in decoding. The books that we choose for our classrooms should represent a variety of artistic styles, ranging from the simplicity and bright color of Lois Ehlert, Tomie de Paola, and Dick Bruna to the detail and complexity of Brian Wildsmith, Susan Jeffers, and Steven Kellog. Books illustrated by photographs offer another sort of artistic experience: Readers of all ages appreciate Tana Hoban's beautiful concept books and the work of Ann Morris in books such as *Bread Bread Bread* and *The Daddy Book.* Children's illustrated picture books offer exquisite examples of watercolor, pastel, collage, and pen-and-ink techniques and can be incorporated into the art curriculum as well. Wordless picture books, like those of John Goodall, tell a story entirely in illustrations. They demand much of the reader and are a good introduction to the active role of the reader in constructing text.

Sometimes the story told in the pictures and the story told in the words are totally dependent upon each other. In Pat Hutchins's *One Hunter,* we see hidden in the bush the animals of which the hunter is oblivious until the last page. Text and illustrations both tell the story. The children see what is happening and what will happen, and can hardly contain their excitement as the number of animals grows. Peggy Rathmann's book *Goodnight Gorilla* has a similar format, as does Pat Hutchins' other classic, *Rosie's Walk.* The reader must interpret the pictures to make full sense of the words.

In the school library resource centre, teachers can find a wide range of enormously attractive hardcover picture books to complement the paperbacks used in the classroom. Children should have as much opportunity as possible to visit the library to select books for their personal reading and for use in the classroom. Careful planning of purchases by teachers and teacher-librarians can ensure that the resources in a school are complementary. Together they can plan for author studies, theme units, and the blending of fiction and nonfiction titles to explore ideas.

### 5. Need

In choosing books for a classroom collection teachers need to consider all the reasons for using books and the contexts in which the books will be used. Ask the questions, "Why am I buying this book? Does it add to what I already have?" Try not to be rushed into buying prepackaged sets, as there may be redundancy and duplication. Look carefully at what you already have and try to identify areas of need before buying new books.

### Guidelines for Building a Comprehensive Collection

To build a comprehensive collection you need:

- **Books at each level of reading difficulty**. For the early stages this includes multiple copies of carefully chosen titles that you will use for guided reading. Identify one or two titles that give you a "benchmark" so that you can recognize the level easily. Try to choose books for guided reading that have varied content, including some nonfiction materials. Build into the collection at each level a variety of types of book and genres. Include folk and fairy tales, nonfiction, stories that reflect the children's own lives, multicultural texts, bilingual or first-language books where appropriate, and books with rich language and poetry.
- **Books which offer you opportunities for teaching children to write**. Choose stories which offer springboards into the children's own experiences and books which have language patterns that can be copied and changed to create easily readable beginning texts. *Mary Wore Her Red Dress and Henry Wore His Green Sneakers, Ten in a Bed, Where's the Bear?* and *Brown Bear, Brown Bear* offer excellent opportunities for children to replicate the patterns.

- **Books which are connected by topic or theme**. Choose several versions of the same story. Fairy tales such as *Red Riding Hood* or *Cinderella* can be found in many versions old and new and representing different cultures. *Aiy Ling Le*, the Chinese Cinderella, and *The Egyptian Cinderella* make interesting comparisons possible. Where possible we include a familiar story in a first language version, (e.g., we have *Lon Po Po*, the Chinese *Little Red Riding Hood*, which is available in both English and Chinese versions).

Series of books also offer opportunities for children to meet the same characters over and over and find connections between stories. For example, the characters in Helen Nicol's *Meg and Mog* books, and Shigeo Watanabe's little bear books make excellent reading material as the predictability of the characters and the plots are part of the fun for young readers. A series such as *The Oxford Reading Tree* has a set of characters who use a magic key as the passport to all kinds of adventures. Stories such as *Nate the Great, The Julian Stories*, and the *Cam Jansen* series for newly independent readers offer security and help develop stamina in reading. This recognition of connections between texts adds to the excitement of reading. Janet and Allan Ahlberg use this interconnectedness to great advantage in *The Jolly Postman* as they refer to familiar fairy-tale characters. The success of the book relies upon the reader's previous knowledge of fairy tales.

Different books by favorite authors, such as Pat Hutchins, John Burningham, Eric Carle, and Sarah Hayes, can also be put together for children to explore. Anthony Browne's books are a great favorite as the illustrations are so unusual and unpredictable.

When buying books a school staff should try to work together, creating a comprehensive and accessible resource base for all the classes. We must provide a wide range of books to meet the needs of readers at all stages of their reading development, as well as books that can be used to create rich programs in all areas of the curriculum. When teachers work together, the chances of building a really successful collection are greatly enhanced.

### How to Group Real Books for Instruction

Real books in primary classroom programs are used in many different ways and for many different purposes. Some of these include:

- read-aloud time, when the teacher reads to the class;
- shared reading, when children and teacher read together;
- guided reading, when a group meets to read together with the teacher;
- independent reading, when children practise reading by themselves;
- partner reading, when children share a book and read together;
- teacher-student conferences, when individual children read aloud to the teacher or talk about a book they have read;
- buddy reading, when children read aloud to a younger or an older buddy;
- read-aloud time, when an older buddy or another adult reads to a child;
- home reading, when children read at home to a parent or sibling;
- home reading, when parents or siblings read aloud to children;
- children reading books to research information;
- children reading books to compare versions;
- children reading books to study the work of one author;
- children reading books on which to model their own stories;
- children listening to tape-recorded stories; and
- children listening to and reading stories on the computer.

The books in the classroom serve all these purposes. It is important that the children see the same books often and in all the reading situations that occur both at school and at home. Therefore, teachers need a wide range of books, and these books need to be organized. Because one of the key components of the program is the child's experience of reading aloud to the teacher in individual and group sessions, teachers need to find books quickly for these conferences. Another significant aspect of the program is the sharing of books at home. When children practise their emerging reading skills at home, it must be with stories that they can read successfully. Again, we need to be able to find books at a certain level quickly. Guided reading sessions must be with material that is chosen very carefully to help a particular group develop strategies.

**It is necessary to sort and group the books in the collection in categories that reflect the stages of reading development through which all children pass.**

We find, by consulting with children in the primary grades and by taking the textual and linguistic features of books into account, that we can group books into a number of categories according to the demands that they make upon the reader. The children help us to compile a collection of books that match their own level of reading independence. They sort and debate putting together books that they can read easily. When the sorting is complete, the children find that if they can read one book in a category — say *Coco Can't Wait* — then it is highly probable that they could read the other books grouped in that category, such as *Just Like Daddy, A Dark, Dark Tale*, and *Whose Mouse Are You?* Using this system, the children can be sure to find a wide selection of books available at their reading level that covers all sorts of topics and ideas. And as teachers, we know where to find the books when we want them.

As we acquire new books for the collection, we decide as a group, the category into which each book must be placed. All books are color-coded so that they can be located easily and replaced after use. Sturdy plastic tool caddies are excellent for storing books and for carrying them to different places in the classroom.

### Categorizing Your Book Collection

There are many possible ways to do this. The following procedure is one that we have found helpful.

1. On your own, or with other teachers in your school, gather together all the books in your classroom.
2. Discard any books that are worn, are of poor quality, or which show bias.
3. Carefully read the descriptions of the features of text described in Chapter Two.
4. Consider the levels described in Chapter Three (Concept Books, Pattern Books, First Steps, etc.). Identify one or two "benchmark" books, which define the level for you. Choose titles which you think are suitable for guided reading and set these aside for obtaining multiple copies.
5. Now, take each book in turn and consider where it fits along the continuum. Look at its main features and place it where you think appropriate.
6. Identify categories by color-coding or some other means — but do

not make these permanent at this stage, as some books will change categories after you read them with children.

7. Test the levelled book collection over several months with the children. Keep a record of the children's behaviors while reading specific books, and note any pertinent observations about the readability level of the books.

8. Review the levels and your notes. Make adjustments to the collection as necessary.

9. Continue to test the collection, moving materials around as necessary.

10. Periodically examine the collection, discarding old books, repositioning others, and adding new books to build an ever more comprehensive set of rich materials for reading.

**In talking about stages and levels we must make it absolutely clear that we do *not* see each stage as discrete.** Children's language learning is never linear. Sometimes there is regression to a previous stage to practise familiar skills and to experience complete control. Sometimes there are leaps ahead, especially when purpose drives the learning. We have seen early readers struggle with difficult text because they really want to find out about dinosaurs or some other important topic. When we think of a child at a particular stage, it is because they are comfortable and confident independent readers with that material. A beginning reader is independent with a concept or wordless picture book, but will read a story like *The Paper Bag Princess* by telling about the pictures.

Another problem we have in talking about stages is that teachers may feel that students should work only with material appropriate for their particular stage of growth. Any system which codes books according to reading level runs into the problem of competitiveness among children and the implication that children at a higher level are superior to those at a lower level. On the contrary, working with literature should mean that children will read widely, as they do at home, from books at all levels of difficulty. The joy of using real books is that we do not restrict the children to one grade-appropriate set of readers. The content of the book is what is important to the child reader, not the reading level. When a wide range of material is available, children move back and forth between the books; sometimes reading the words, sometimes reading only the key words, sometimes reading only the pictures. They will choose very wisely to practise their independent reading skills with books that offer them the least difficulty, but they will enjoy looking at pictures in books at all levels.

We have learned that a successful reading experience for young children, when they try to read independently, is the result of an interaction between their determination to read *this* book on *this* occasion, the skills and strategies for decoding that they bring to this endeavor, and the demands of the text itself. What we are trying to do as teachers is help make the most effective match that we can between the reading abilities of the students and the demands that are made upon them by the text. When a child brings a book to us, or takes a book home to read to a parent, we want the child to experience as much success and as little frustration as possible. The organization of the books into stages allows us to help children find a number of books that are all more or less similar in terms of their textual difficulty.

Finally, a word about ages and grades. We expect our children to develop as readers in kindergarten, Grade 1, and Grade 2. Most will be independent by late Grade 2. Some will come to Grade 1 already reading. The whole point of a program that uses real books is that it allows us the needed flexibility to meet the individual needs of the children in the class, whatever their ages and abilities. The children we are describing in this book are in kindergarten, Grade 1, and Grade 2 classrooms. The ways in which we respond to them in the reading situation depends on *what they can do* and, therefore, *what they need to know next* to develop as enthusiastic readers. The program is the same whatever the grade. The difference between a Grade 2 and a kindergarten class lies, of course, in the number of fluent independent readers, the types of books they read and we read, and the depth and amount of written responses that we expect from the children.

The following chart may be used when selecting books at the bookstore or in the library as a quick guide to where a book fits on the continuum of reading development. This chart is based on the levels of difficulty defined in Chapter Three and is matched to the three early stages of reading development.

Teachers can create a poster of this chart for the classroom so children can learn how to make selections based on their level of ability. They will begin to learn how the levels work and what makes a book easier or harder to read. They will begin to recommend books to each other based not only on their enjoyment of the story, but also on the ease of reading.

| BEGINNING READERS | | | |
|---|---|---|---|
| Features of the Book | Concept Books | Pattern Books | First Steps |
| size of print | large, clear, separate from illustrations | large, clear, separate from illustrations | relatively large, well spaced |
| number of words on a page | one word or very short phrase | one sentence on a page | one sentence on every page |
| match between words and pictures | perfect match | one picture matching one sentence | vocabulary easily predictable from pictures |
| repetition of sentences or refrains | possibly | strong rhythms and linguistic pattern | simple story to tell but sentences may have different structures |
| rhyming words | rarely | strong predictable rhymes | rhyme at the end of sentences |
| vocabulary from children's oral language | number words, color words, animals... | words familiar to children; short; frequently used | words still drawn from everyday usage |
| content is familiar to children | alphabet, counting, color, familiar objects | color, animals, home, family, counting | doing things, everyday experiences |
| special features | mixture of upper and lower case | only one word changes from page to page | possibly describes sequence of events |

| DEVELOPING READER | | | |
|---|---|---|---|
| Features of the Book | Step a Little Further | Step a Little Faster | Taking Off |
| size of print | relatively well spaced; clear | may be smaller; books are getting longer | more print; smaller; more closely spaced |
| number of words on a page | one or two sentences on a page | more than one sentence on a page | several sentences |
| match between words and pictures | one picture; meaningful match | pictures help reader predict specific vocabulary | pictures add to the text and may provide clues |
| repetition of sentences or refrains | random but not systematic | frequent repetition of an idea or phrase | more formal properties of written language |
| rhyming words | rhymes may occur | possibly strong rhymes or rhythms | may be a feature |
| vocabulary from children's oral language | words still close to children's own vocabulary | more unusual or difficult vocabulary | moving away from everyday structures |
| content is familiar to children | events from a child's experience | moving beyond personal everyday experience | content may be imaginary or humorous |
| special features | may be a question and answer format | introduction of character and sequence of events; fantasy and imagination | fantasy ; ridiculous situations; humor; more abstract concepts |

| FLUENT READERS | | | |
|---|---|---|---|
| **Features of the Book** | **You're Away** | **Getting Longer** | **First Novels** |
| size of print | more text; smaller print | print is not large | print is not large |
| number of words on a page | stories are longer; paragraphs may be used | paragraph structure; longer stories resemble novels | paragraph structure; ideas carried from page to page |
| match between words and pictures | still a picture on every page which enhances text; | still a picture on every page; may add information not in the words | may have one or two pictures |
| repetition of sentences or refrains | used stylistically for a specific effect; less assistance for the reader | style of writing increasingly literary; not significant for decoding | not significant |
| rhyming words | less assistance for reader from rhyme | not significant | not significant |
| vocabulary from children's oral language | language has more definite literary quality; may use metaphor, etc. | written forms take precedence over oral; vocabulary more sophisticated | written forms take precedence over oral; vocabulary more sophisticated |
| content is familiar to children | wide variety of topics and universal themes appear in text | thoughts and themes familiar but wide variety | thoughts and themes familiar but wide variety |
| special features | powerful emotional hook from illustration and text | challenging picture books that may have the format of a novel | chapters; may have sub-plots and many characters |

THREE  ❧

# How Reading Development Progresses

## The Three Stages of Reading Development

Reading Conferences with individual children and Guided Reading Groups are the two contexts in which the classroom teacher assesses reading progress and offers direct help to the child, mediating between the reader and the text. With experience, the teacher can recognize the characteristics of the stage of reading development for a particular child at any one time. When the teacher recognizes what a child knows and understands the developmental sequence of reading acquisition, the teacher can scaffold instruction to offer the next piece of the puzzle and give the most appropriate support; support that will advance the learning while allowing the child to feel in control.

There are three broad stages which we believe characterize the normal child's developmental progress in the primary years. Though the speed with which children pass through these stages varies, it is generally the case that there is a common progression through the stages. Put very simply, there is the stage of beginning or emergent literacy, when some of the purposes for reading and the reading behaviors are understood, but few of the strategies for independent reading are in place. Secondly, we talk about developing readers — those children who have some strategies and a growing sense of themselves as readers. Thirdly, the young fluent readers in the primary years have "cracked the code" and now continue to refine their understandings, build vocabulary, and respond in ever more sophisticated ways to the nuances of texts.

Table 3.1 shows how we organized our collection of literature in the classrooms into levels, or categories, that correspond to the three stages, thus ensuring **that a child reading independently and aloud will experience success with these books**. As well, the levels facilitate use of the books for direct instruction in reading conferences and guided reading groups.

**Table 3.1**

| Stage | Level/Category of Books |
|-------|------------------------|
| Beginning Reader | Concept Books, Pattern Books, and First Stories |
| Developing Reader | Step a Little Further, Step a Little Faster, and Taking Off |
| Fluent Independent Reader | You're Away, Getting Longer, First Novels |

In this chapter we show how the reading levels of the books correspond to the stages of development of the children and how to use the books.

## Stage One: The Beginning Readers and Their Books

These are our very youngest children who have had the least experience with reading. Children at this stage may or may not realize that the words on the page correspond to the talk that comes from a reader's lips. They tell stories with great gusto and read pictures, but they have rudimentary concepts about print. These children may not know the meaning of the words we use to refer to print, such as *letter*, *sound*, and *sentence*. When they bring a book to share with the teacher, it is the adult who will do most of the reading. The child will chime in with predictable parts or predict words at the ends of sentences. When they write, these children experiment with letters and sounds and may represent words with symbols other than letters. Their writing may look like scribble.

When Carla was the doctor in the Doctor's Centre, she wrote this prescription for her patient.

OTUKOROB
ROTSSLIEB

Playing at being a travel agent, Joshua wrote this plane ticket for his client.

As beginning readers progress and develop alphabetic knowledge, they may represent words with appropriate salient sounds. They become phonetic writers, basing their representations of letter sounds on what they hear and representing each syllable by one letter, as shown in this writing by Rosalie.

DA t S B
S r +

The truck is big
It's red too!

Previous experience with a book is very important at this stage for successful reading. After two or three encounters with an easy-to-read pattern book, a child will memorize patterns and chant the text from memory. The concept of word-to-sound correspondence is still not fully established and, even when finger-pointing, they can easily lose their place. Frequent repetition of the same text builds confidence, a feeling of success, and a familiarity with the habit of reading. It also helps to develop awareness of the one-to-one correspondence of print to sound. The eye becomes accustomed to the left-to-right sweep of print on a page. The child becomes an expert at page-turning and following a story from beginning to end. Parents often say to us, " But they're only memorizing." Our reply is, "Yes, isn't it great that they've reached this stage? Now we are going to look at some simple stories together that will move them on to more complex reading strategies."

Use the checklist on pages 55-56 to assess the progress of beginning readers. When most of the attributes of this stage are in place, a student is ready to move to the next stage, that of the Developing Reader.

### Concept Books

These books have one word or a very short phrase and a picture. The words and picture match perfectly. Usually these books simply label a concept or an object. Alphabet books and counting books fall into this category. Jan Pienkowski has written and illustrated a visually appealing series that names *Colors, Homes,* and *Time* among others. Such books can be used as first dictionaries by children at a later stage. Very occasionally we find a book in this category that also tells a story, such as Pat Hutchins's *One Hunter,* Byron Barton's *Where's Al?* and Peggy Rathmann's *Goodnight Gorilla,* but the narrative is contained in the pictures and not in the words. Using books such as these, beginning readers can experience instant success and begin to see the printed word as having a meaningful relationship with a picture.

### Wordless Picture Books

Wordless picture books are a special kind of concept book. Telling a story from pictures is part of reading and practising this with these books develops both story sense and book-handling skills. These books offer a chance to explore story structure and detail in illustrations.

John Goodall has a series of books in this category, and one of our favorites is *Up and Up* by Shirley Hughes. These books can also be used in increasingly sophisticated ways, for drama and story writing. How-

# Characteristics of the Beginning Reader and Writer

**Name:**_____ **Date:** _____

## Knowledge of Literacy

The child understands:

| | YES | NO | SOME-TIMES |
|---|---|---|---|
| that reading is meaning making — expects print to make sense; | | | |
| • that writing is talk written down; | | | |
| • that print holds meaning and conveys information; | | | |
| • that reading is a worthwhile skill to achieve; | | | |
| • that books are enjoyable; | | | |
| • that books will be about something related to the pictures. | | | |

## Reading Behavior

The child:

| | YES | NO | SOME-TIMES |
|---|---|---|---|
| • likes to listen to stories, rhymes, poems | | | |
| • has favorite stories, can't miss a word of old favorites; | | | |
| • "role plays" self as a reader, likes to look at books, handles books voluntarily; | | | |
| • knows how to hold a book and turn the pages one at a time, front to back | | | |
| • reads pictures and knows you can predict meaning from them. Draws on prior knowledge to "read"; | | | |
| • understands print directionality. Words in English start on the left and move to the right, and go from top to bottom; | | | |
| • can show you words; | | | |
| • knows where to find title and author's name; | | | |
| • knows where a story begins and ends; | | | |

| | YES | NO | SOME-TIMES |
|---|---|---|---|
| • tries to read environmental print, knows some words by sight such as own name and names of family members; | | | |
| • reads pattern books, memorizes them holistically; | | | |
| • relies heavily on picture clues and on language patterns to aid memorization of text; | | | |
| • can hear rhyme; | | | |
| • matches beginning and final sounds accurately; | | | |
| • does not read word for word; | | | |
| • can retell the main events of the story; | | | |
| • reads at a literal level; | | | |
| • borrows materials to read to others. | | | |

## Writing Behavior

These descriptors are shown as a continuum. Children move from random scribbling to representing words with letters.

| The child: | YES | NO | SOME-TIMES |
|---|---|---|---|
| • scribbles and plays with paper and pencil; | | | |
| • uses arbitrary symbols to represent sounds or words; | | | |
| • uses letters to represent sounds and words but without sound-letter accuracy; | | | |
| • writes without spacing; | | | |
| • hears only one major sound in a word; | | | |
| • hears more than one sound in a word; | | | |
| • knows names of letters in sequence; | | | |
| • recognizes individual letters and can say their names; | | | |
| • has beginnings of accurate sound-letter accuracy, knows some letters by sound and by name. | | | |

ever, as we want children to become familiar with *print*, the use of wordless books in teaching reading is perhaps limited.

### Pattern Books

With their very strong rhythms and linguistic patterns, these books are the most important part of our collection for beginning readers. Usually one sentence and one picture appear on a page, and only one word changes from page to page. The most famous and perfect of all pattern books is *Brown Bear, Brown Bear What Do You See?* by Bill Martin Jr. and Eric Carle. Prereading children become instantly familiar with the pattern and "read" the story with great enthusiasm. They do not yet make an accurate sound-to-print match, but they are surely reading! *The Cat on the Mat* series, published by Oxford University Press and written by Brian Wildsmith, offers some perfect pattern books. Look, too, at the early stages of the published reading programs for many wonderful titles. The *PM Starters* from Scholastic are one good example of this sort of material.

### Poetry

Nursery rhymes and poems are extremely important reading for beginning readers. They memorize rhymes and read them to themselves. They develop an ear for the rhythms and cadences of language. The roots of a love of poetry begin with Mother Goose, so traditional rhymes play a large part in the language program. There is strong evidence that children who experience lots of poetry and rhyme develop phonemic awareness — the ability to recognize sounds within words — which is crucial for success in reading. (Adams 1990)

Poetry can be written on charts and posted on the walls for reading and rereading. Beginning readers can listen to poetry on tape while following the text with the eyes. Most teachers have their favorite poems and usually link poems to themes and times of the year. Creating our own poetry anthologies, based on shared poetry experiences, is part of how we build and maintain a vibrant collection. Children can collect their own favorite rhymes in a personal anthology and bring it to read to us. Our own personal collections of favorite poems, written in a hardback notebook, are a favorite choice for independent reading in our classrooms.

*First Steps*

Books in this category have a picture and a sentence on every page. Sentence structures may be repeated throughout the book, or they may change from page to page as new information is introduced. The books have a simple story to tell, and the vocabulary is easily predictable from the pictures. The print is relatively large and well-spaced. Children can read these simple stories with the help of an adult or by themselves if it is not their first experience with the book. They will read the pictures, chime in with ends of sentences or with repetitions, and will learn how to turn pages and look for the printed word.

*Pumpkin, Pumpkin* by Jeanne Titherington is a wonderful example of this sort of book. The text is simple — a single sentence broken into clauses, each clause with its own soft, detailed illustration drawn with pencil crayons. On the first page is a picture of Jamie's hand holding a single pumpkin seed. He plants the seed and watches it grow. On the last page he shows us the six seeds he saves from his pumpkin for planting in the spring. The text is predictable and simple but the book is a delightful introduction for young children to the cycle of life and growth. Jamie is watched in his garden by many small creatures who are not mentioned in the text but who are part of the book nevertheless. We have enjoyed this book with many beginning readers who have found the rhythm of the language easy to read. This is a great book for Halloween or springtime reading.

Another very popular First Steps book is *Dinosaurs, Dinosaurs* by Byron Barton. The repetitive sentence structures coupled with the brightly colored illustrations make this book compelling reading.

## Stage Two: The Developing Readers and Their Books

Children at this stage have made a breakthrough. This is the stage at which they pester people constantly to hear them read. They know that each printed word is separate and corresponds to one spoken word. They can find isolated words on a page, point to first letters, and follow print accurately across the page. They read books they know with accuracy. They frequently finger point to keep their place and are developing a small sight vocabulary. They use picture clues and possibly initial consonants to help decode unknown words. When they write these children use vowels as well as consonants, though not always the accurate vowel. They spell using phonics, understanding that letters in combination make certain sounds. At this stage they may have introduced spacing into their writing.

I U Sed LAZY to MAKEM STRUC+ SePt 17 1991

This writing sample from Meng, written after working for some time on a complicated building structure, explains what materials he used. His emerging skill in composition is shown by his use of spaces and some conventional spellings for the more common function words (to, I, my), and by his ability to identify correctly, for the most part, the dominant sound in individual words.

We might say that these children have pole-vaulted into reading. Sometimes a very dramatic change occurs in their reading and it seems to happen overnight: They go home one day unable to read and come to school the next day with a whole new outlook on the process! The begin to pull together all the strategies they have been learning, and they now use a combination of semantic, syntactic, and phonic cues to decode words they don't know. They have a developed sight vocabulary and, when they write, they space their words and use vowels.

Der Mrg Muzumjar
Thac for Halpino us with are
Mars I ic wrking wit
frpm h uwu

Elana's thank-you letter to a parent for helping her class with their maps shows her beginning mastery of conventional spelling, as demonstrated.

Use the checklist on pages 60-61 to assess and monitor the progress of the developing readers in your class.

While they know *how* to read, developing readers lack the stamina needed for novels and still need the support of pictures, clearly printed text, and familiar vocabulary. They read most easily from books that have familiar content, though they are able to attempt unfamiliar words. They may decode a word without knowing what it means. The following categories of books offer them a diverse choice of reading material.

# Characteristics of the Developing Reader and Writer

**Name:**_____ **Date:** _____

| **Knowledge of Literacy**<br><br>The child understands: | YES | NO | SOME-TIMES |
|---|---|---|---|
| • that reading and writing are meaningful; | | | |
| • that they can use reading and writing for their own purposes in many contexts; | | | |
| • that they are successful as readers and writers; | | | |
| • that readers use strategies to unlock unknown words; | | | |
| • that prediction based on meaning is the most important strategy; | | | |

| **Reading Behavior**<br><br>The child: | YES | NO | SOME-TIMES |
|---|---|---|---|
| • reads familiary pattern books and simple picture books fluently; | | | |
| • continues to enjoy being read to; | | | |
| • begins to widen choice of materials; | | | |
| • reads other children's work; | | | |
| • uses picture and meaning clues first; | | | |
| • develops strategies for unlocking unknown words but needs help; | | | |
| • begins to self-correct when meaning is lost, re-reads to find meaning;; | | | |
| • doesn't give up easily, tackles new material with adult support; | | | |
| • reads slowly and haltingly, word by word; | | | |

| | YES | NO | SOME-TIMES |
|---|---|---|---|
| • reads out loud for the most part but may read silently with familiar print; | | | |
| • begins to use phonic clues; | | | |
| knows that letters are important (recognizes that bed and bad are different words): | | | |
| knows consonants and consonant digraphs; | | | |
| blends consonants together; | | | |
| knows long vowel sounds; | | | |
| • has developed a bank of words known by sight; | | | |
| • borrows materials to read to others. | | | |

| **Writing Behavior**<br>The child: | YES | NO | SOME-TIMES |
|---|---|---|---|
| • uses writing for different purposes — personal story, non-fiction, poetry; | | | |
| • knows stories have a beginning, middle, and end; | | | |
| • begins to include dialogue — uses the language of books; | | | |
| • uses both consonants and vowels to represent sounds; | | | |
| • spells some high-frequency words correctly; | | | |
| • begins to use spaces between words; | | | |
| • produces writing that can be read by others; | | | |
| • represents every syllable in a word; | | | |
| • conferences with a friend; | | | |
| • is willing to add more to writing; | | | |
| • edits a few words more independently; | | | |
| • begins to use personal dictionary. | | | |

### Step a Little Further

Books in this category are similar in structure to the "First Steps" books. They tell a story; they have print which is relatively well-spaced; there is a picture and only one or two sentences on a page. The vocabulary and the concepts may be unusual or more difficult, but the language structures are close to the oral language patterns of young children, and the stories usually concern events that are familiar from a child's experience.

Some of the favorites in this category are *Just Like Daddy* by Frank Asch, *Across the Stream* by Mirra Ginsburg and Nancy Tafuri (notable for its lovely large print and the ryhming structure), and *How Do I Put It On?,* the first in the series by Shigeo Watanabe about a little bear. This last title is a book that is made easy to read by its syntactic structure. The story is told in the form of question and answer. "Do I put it on like this?" asks the bear with his cap on his foot. The children use the syntactic cuing system together with the picture to supply the answer. "No! I put my cap on my head."

### Step a Little Faster

Books in this category have pictures which still provide most of the information needed to tell the story. The pictures help the reader predict specific vocabulary in the text. Help may also be available in the form of strong rhymes or rhythms or in the frequent repetition of an idea or phrase. These books are longer than those in the "Step a Little Further" section and more complex. There is more than one sentence on a page, the print may be smaller, and the vocabulary may be more difficult or unusual.

Children need a little more stamina to achieve independence with these books. One of our favorites is *Each Peach Pear Plum* by Janet and Allan Ahlberg. Each page introduces a new nursery rhyme or storybook character hidden in an unusual place. The children love to point out where they all are! The success they have with this book often leads them to try *The Jolly Postman* even though the words in that book are much more difficult to read. The Ahlberg fans in the class will read the book and the letters it contains from story characters and will find all the intertextual references that the authors have deliberately included.

*Taking Off*

Books in this category have considerably more print on a page. The print may be smaller or more closely spaced on the page, or may be presented in an unusual format. The syntactic patterns may be beginning to move away from everyday structures and to take on the more formal properties of written language. *Peepo!* (again by the Ahlbergs), *Mr. Magnolia* by Quentin Blake, *Frog and Toad Are Friends* by Arnold Lobel, and *Peace At Last* by Jill Murray are books that can now be read fluently. Remember, though, that all these books have been enjoyed at previous stages. *Peepo!* is a wonderful book to share with prereaders, because they read "Peepo!" every time it appears, while you read the rest of the text.

## Stage Three: The Fluent Independent Readers and Their Books

Children at this stage can read well. They have developed some stamina and can now read silently. They are developing the habit of reading and can talk about the books they have read. They begin to read longer books and first novels. As writers, these children use standard spelling except when tackling a long, difficult word.

There are many picture books that are suitable in content and style for these children, as well as books that look more like novels. The books in the next categories help children make the transition from picture books to first novels and lead the newly independent reader into the world of full-length books. Children at this stage are building vocabulary, becoming increasingly strategic in their use of the cuing systems, and learning to deepen their response to stories. They learn to read for information and to use that information to write factual books and reports.

*You're Away*

Books in this category still have a picture on every page, but there is more text and the print is smaller. The stories are longer and the literary quality of the language is more apparent. Many books at this stage begin to address issues that may be important to young children. There is less assistance for the reader from rhyme or repetition. Some favorite books in this category are *Gorilla* by Anthony Browne; *Corduroy*, a story about a lonely little girl's relationship with her father, by Don Freeman; and *The Snowy Day* by Ezra Jack Keats.

---

1. Does it turtles have the saem color?

2. Where do females lay eggs?

3. Most turtles are green and brown and black. But some has red, orange, yellow and dots and lines.

✓ 4. Do real turtles talk?
   No because turtles reptiles not human beings.

5. Do real turtles have friends?

6. Franklin talks to polar bears do real turtle talk to polar bears? the

✓ 7. Do turtles live in snow?
   No Because it too cold.

✓ 8. Do real turtles have there own room like Franklin? No becdse they live in there shell.

9. Do real turtles sleep like Franklin? their

✓ 10. Can real turtles sit down? walk or
    No turtles walk with four feet.

11. How many egg dose a green sea turtle lay?
    100

12. Do real turtle drink water?

13. Is Franklin a real turtle?
    No because he is fiction he is not real.

---

After reading many books about a turtle named Franklin, and exploring some nonfiction material about turtles, Christopher developed this preliminary list of questions and answers. In this first draft he struggles with the concept of a question. The check marks indicate the questions he will use to make a trivia game for his classmates.

*Getting Longer*

These stories require some stamina on the part of the reader. Not only is there more print on a page, but the stories are longer and more complex. The vocabulary is more sophisticated; however, most of these books still make the print digestible by having a picture on every page and by focusing on thoughts and themes familiar to young children. The writing may be literary in style. This category includes some of the more challenging picture books as well as some that have the format of novels. For example, *The Whispering Cloth — A Refugee's Story; Mr. Putter and Tabby Series*; Bill Cosby's "Little Bill Books" with such titles as *The Best Way to Play* and *The Meanest Thing to Say*, are books which fit well into this category.

*First Novels*

This category continues to make demands on the reader in terms of the length of the books, the size and quantity of print on a page, and the thought-provoking nature of the content. The author's message is carried primarily by the text although there may be a few well-placed illustrations to break the density of the print. Most of these books feature chapters or a collection of short stories. It takes more than one reading to finish one of these books. *Grandpa Chatterji*, the *Amber Brown* books, *Skylark*, and *Buddy, The First Seeing Eye Dog* are examples of this category.

## Other Reading Materials for Your Classroom

As well as housing this range of fiction, a well-equipped primary classroom will have other reading material available for different purposes. The following materials should be represented:

- audio-visual materials, including books and tapes;
- computer software;
- children's own published writing;
- reference books;
- dictionaries and encyclopedias;
- first language materials where appropriate;
- maps and atlases;
- puzzle and quiz books;

- magazines, comics, catalogues, and newspapers;
- posters, labels, and notices; and
- greetings cards.

Given all these resources, the next question to be addressed is how to use them. What do we do when we are listening to children read at their different growth points? How do we use a book with a beginning reader, and how do we use the same book with a fluent reader? How do we organize the classroom so that young children may have the maximum opportunity to engage in genuine acts of reading and writing? How do we teach reading and writing using real books?

# FOUR

# Exploring Books With Children

Young children have many different interactions with books, at home and at school, all of which contribute to their growing store of information about how print works. They hear books read aloud, both individually and as members of a group. The child listens as someone reads and becomes absorbed in the story. If the read-aloud experience is accompanied by an opportunity to see the words as they are read, then the child may make connections between the words they hear and the visual display of words on the page. There are several ways to provide this experience. The child can sit on the adult's lap and follow the text in a small book, or can sit alone, listening to a tape-recorded story while reading along in his or her own book. Children may watch the pages of a "big book" turn or see the words on an overhead screen as the teacher reads to the class. Some computer software, such as *Wiggle Works*, also allows students to view a familiar story, hear the story read aloud, and read the story for themselves simultaneously. Many teachers find this experience particularly beneficial for E.S.L. students, as they become completely immersed in the story.

## Shared Reading and Writing Sessions

Shared reading can take place with the whole class or with a small group. Use a big book or a language experience chart to demonstrate concepts about print and strategies for reading to the children. The teacher provides scaffolding for the children so that they can experience success. A chart or a big book is used so that everyone can see the words and the teacher may use a pointer to indicate words or letters.

Here are some ideas for making shared reading sessions valuable learning experiences for young children.

1. Make the reading process explicit by describing what you are doing. Before beginning to read the book, talk about the cover. What is this going to be about?
2. Turn the pages and talk about the pictures; predict the meaning; highlight some key vocabulary in your talk.
3. Read the book once through for enjoyment.
4. Talk about what happened. What was the story/poem/chart about? What experience did the stories remind them of?
5. What was the best part? Did the children like it? Discuss their reactions.
6. Read again. On this and subsequent rereadings, choose one or two of the following ideas. Remember, don't keep young children sitting in a group for too long. Be sure you choose concepts that are appropriate for their developmental level and learning needs.

- Ask the children to predict what is going to happen next by looking at the pictures. Always ask, "How do you know?"
- Talk about details in pictures. Ask, "What emotions are the characters showing? Where is this taking place? How do you know?"
- Stop at the end of a line or before a key word such as a character's name, a repeating phrase, or a rhyming word and let the children chime in.
- Cover the last word of a line or a key word and let the children chime in. Ask, "How did you know that?"
- Show the first letter of a key word and let the children chime in.
- Ask children to find words in the text and point to them.
- Show how the pages turn when you get to the end of the writing.
- Point to the words as they move from left to right.

Maximize Shared Writing with the following ideas.

- Ask the children what words they think should be written;
- Talk as you write; show how the letters are formed;
- Talk about the sounds the letters make;
- Talk about punctuation: capital letters, periods, question marks, and commas; and
- When the message is finished, have the children read it together.

## Independent Private Reading

Children also read alone or with a friend when no adult is present. In this case they practise their independent reading, making what sense they can of words and pictures without mediation. They explore books in this context much as adults do when they read, skipping bits that are less interesting, moving back and forth in the text to check things out, abandoning a book before the end if it seems uninteresting or too difficult, or repeatedly reading something that seems fascinating. During independent practice children will browse through books that are too difficult to read, enjoying the pictures, and perhaps reading captions in nonfiction material. They will also return to books they know and which they can read with confidence, books they have learned by listening to them read aloud, or to which they have been introduced in the guided reading conference.

The balanced classroom literacy program provides read-aloud, shared reading, and independent reading opportunities for children to have encounters with books. But it also provides a fourth and crucial opportunity for children to learn to read. **The more frequently young children practise their reading by reading aloud individually, or in very small groups with a caring adult, the more easily they become independent readers and writers**. It is our job as reading teachers to organize opportunities for children to practise reading while we offer the appropriate amount of support. In these reading conferences, or guided reading sessions, we can ensure that we offer the right support at the right time, modifying the responses we make so that the children gain the most from the experience. We scaffold the instruction, gauging how much help to give, which strategies to teach, and which concepts about reading to introduce or reinforce.

## Guided Reading

Guided Reading sessions, or Reading Conferences, can be held with individuals or with small groups. Our preference is for individual conferences, which are more intimate, more focused, and usually richer in teaching possibilities. However, the classroom is a busy place and time is limited. It may be more productive for teachers to organize children to read in groups of four, and to structure the day such that several groups read each day and all children read at least twice a week. If reading groups are formed, it will still be necessary to hold individual conferences now and then to check on developing skills and to give each child the individual attention that builds a close relationship between teacher and child.

### Forming Groups for Guided Reading

Guided Reading Groups offer the teacher the opportunity to teach a group of children whose needs are similar. It allows children to practise skills using books that are neither too easy nor too difficult with other children who are at the same level. However, there needs to be a continuous forming and re-forming of such groups so that the danger of creating "high " and "low" groups is avoided. Nothing is more damaging to progress than to be part of the "low readers' group," and the danger of creating ability groups is well documented. The classroom needs to be a place where children are called into groups which are different on various occasions, not fixed and labelled. Small guided reading groups, composed of children who need similar instruction using the same level of text, should be changed frequently as the children's ability develops. This means that teachers must be constantly assessing and reassessing children's ability and must respond to change as it occurs. No group should stay together for more than about six weeks as it becomes static and children can become "labelled."

Groups which are heterogeneous in terms of reading ability can be formed for other purposes, such as responding to literature, researching a topic, planning a Readers' Theatre presentation, as well as for a host of other classroom activities. This helps to avoid labelling children as belonging to a certain group.

*Choosing Books for Guided Reading*

The book which is chosen for the guided reading session is determined by the childrens' needs at the time, the material that is available, and the purpose that the teacher sets for the session. As far as possible the teacher tries to match the material to the instructional level of the children so that they are able to read most of the text, but are also presented with some challenges that stretch their thinking and require them to use their developing reading strategies. If children are comfortably reading easy pattern books, then it would be appropriate to choose a book from the "First Steps" list. Readers who are fluent and comfortable with "First Steps" books would work with a title from "Step a Little Further," and so on. The ease with which a beginning reader reads a particular text depends upon its familiarity, their comfort in the reading situation, and their motivation. Finding a book that offers just the right amount of challenge is sometimes difficult. We want to offer the opportunity for new strategies to be introduced as children tackle unfamiliar words, but we also want to find books that children will enjoy and find interesting.

The intrinsic interest of the text is a key factor, and it is important that the texts chosen for guided reading should be satisfying to read and offer plenty of stimulus for conversation. The talk around the story is of as much importance as the decoding of the words. A really good book will offer plenty of opportunities for discussion, especially around word meanings. When children let a story stimulate their thinking and their imagination, there is the chance to develop rich oral language. This is especially important for an increasing number of children in classrooms for whom English is a new language. The guided reading group is a place where vocabulary and language structures in English may be learned and practised. Punctuation offers clues to the reader for expression and phrasing and, in guided reading sessions, reading the punctuation can also be a focus for learning, which is especially helpful for second language learners.

These groups really become exciting when there is some concrete experience which can be related to the book, such as handling real objects, using physical actions, and experiencing events in the world outside the classroom. A trip to the park, for example, can generate language about play, language which can be recorded by the teacher. In a guided reading session that uses a book about going to the park, the same language will be encountered again. For new English learners this matching of concrete experience to spoken and written language is of vital importance. A small collection of objects that are found in a story can be assembled and shown to the children before the story is read. They can use the objects to predict the story and to learn vocabulary. For each of the Guided Reading Lesson Plans we have prepared (pages 77, 79, 81, 84), we have suggested some objects that could be collected for this purpose.

If children are reading in groups, it is essential that each child has a copy of the book. The teacher needs to obtain multiple copies of those books which are to be used for group work. In each category or level we choose some texts which are suitable for group work and which seem to offer the most in terms of reading instruction. We have our favorite titles at each level that we like to work with. Multiple copies of books are packaged together in resealable plastic bags and kept separate from the main collection. Another copy of each of these books needs to be in the collection for children to browse, because after the book has been read in a guided reading session, the children will want to return to it to practise their independent reading. They may also want to borrow a copy to take home and read to their parents.

The following titles are particularly rewarding to work with at each level.

**Concept Books**
*Goodnight Gorilla* – Peggy Rathmann
*One Hunter* – Pat Hutchins
*Eating the Alphabet* – Lois Ehlert
*Fish Eyes* –Lois Ehlert
*K is for Kiss Goodnight* – Jill Sardegna

**Pattern Books**
*Cat on the Mat* – Brian Wildsmith
*I Can Count* – Denise Lewis Patrick
*Dear Zoo* – Rod Campbell
*Brown Bear, Brown Bear, What Do You See?* – Bill Martin Jr. and Eric Carle
*I Went Walking* – Sue Williams

**First Steps**
*Dinosaurs, Dinosaurs* – Byron Barton
*I Like Books* – Anthony Browne

*Four Black Puppies* – Sally Grindley
*Not Now Bernard* – David McKee
*Pumpkin, Pumpkin* – Jeanne Titherington
*If I Were You* – Brian Wildsmith
*See What I Can Do* – Denise Lewis Patrick

## Step a Little Further
*The Last Puppy* – Frank Asch
*A Dark Dark Tale* – Ruth Brown
*The Chick and the Duckling* – Mirra Ginsburg
*Coco Can't Wait* – Taro Gomi
*This is the Bear* – Sarah Hayes
*Whose Mouse Are You?* – Robert Kraus
*Mouse Paint* – Ellen Stoll Walsh
*How Do I Put It On?* – Shigeo Watanabe

## Step a Little Faster
*Each Peach Pear Plum* – Janet and Allan Ahlberg
*Who Sank the Boat?* – Pamela Allen
*The Very Hungry Caterpillar* – Eric Carle
*George Shrinks* – Willaim Joyce
*Leo the Late Bloomer* – Robert Kraus
*Meg and Mog* – Helen Nicoll
*My Cat Likes to Hide in Boxes* – Eve Sutton

## Taking Off
*Peepo!* – Janet and Allan Ahlberg
*Mr. Gumpy's Outing* – John Burningham
*The Secret Birthday Message* – Eric Carle
*Frog and Toad are Friends* – Arnold Lobel
*Peace at Last* – Jill Murray

## You're Away
*Gorilla* – Anthony Browne
*Willy the Wimp* – Anthony Browne
*The Very Grouchy Ladybug* – Eric Carle
*Wilfred Gordon MacDonald Partridge* – Mem Fox
*The Snowy Day* – Ezra Jack Keats
*When I Was Young in the Mountains* – Cynthia Rylant
*Where the Wild Things Are* – Maurice Sendak
*John Brown, Rose and the Midnight Cat* – Jenny Wagner

**Getting Longer**

*The Jolly Postman* – Janet & Allan Ahlberg
*The Pain and the Great One* – Judy Blume
*The Hockey Sweater* – Roch Carrier
*Chang's Paper Pony* – Eleanor Coerr
*Miss Rumphius* – Barbara Cooney
*Dr. DeSoto* – William Steig

**First Novels**

*Flat Stanley* – Jeff Brown
*The Fantastic Mr. Fox* – Roald Dahl
*The Shrinking of Treehorn* – Florence Parry Heide
*The Iron Man* – Ted Hughes
*Sarah Plain and Tall* – Patricia MacLachlan

Publishers' programs also offer ways of creating sets of books which are levelled and progressive in the demands they make on young readers. In purchasing these programs look for titles that are good to order in sets. Many publishers have now packaged their programs to reflect several levels of difficulty — as many as twenty — before the texts become suitable for young fluent readers. In our view, it is probably not necessary to classify the classroom collection in such detail. Our categories recognize a general progression from level to level that makes sense for the children we teach and for us in managing the collection. We find the notion of twenty separate categories overwhelming and unnecessary for the regular classroom, and we prefer to work with fewer distinctions. For children in remedial reading programs teachers will make smaller distinctions between levels of difficulty, but the majority of children do not need to progress in such small increments. Consequently, we would need to combine publishers' levels to reflect our own categories.

Watch, too, for older anthologies which may be in your school and which may offer excellent literature for guided reading groups. These may not be organized by levels of difficulty that correspond to the levels you are creating with your resources, so it is important to consider each individual story or poem and see where it fits in your program. Refer to Table 3.1 on page 52 as a guide.

In choosing literature for your reading groups, remember that *you* must like the books, too. Buy sets of books that you want to work with because they give you opportunities to explore ideas with children.

The ideas in the books are as important as the textual support that is offered to the reader. Choose books first and foremost because reading them is a satisfying experience.

*What We Teach*

When we bring children to us for a focused and structured reading time together, we want to scaffold our instruction so that they can value and successfully use what they know already, while they are introduced to new learning at the same time. Within the three broad levels of reading development that we use to describe growth, there are of course many subtle and complicated differences from one child to another. One may be learning more visually, relying on visual patterns in words and recognizing words by sight. Another may be developing faster as a user of phonemic patterns, able to break words into onsets and rimes. No two children are exactly the same. We recognize that within each of our levels there will be some children who are just entering this stage, and some who are about to leave it. We stress the importance of being flexible with the children and of keeping records of books read and strategies discussed. The analysis of children's reading at key points during the school year is an essential part of knowing where they are in their reading development and determining in which group to place them. This analysis can be accomplished through the use of checklists, such as the ones in Chapter Three, or by carrying out a "Running Record."

A "Running Record" is a technique developed by Marie Clay and fully described in her book *An Observation Survey of Early Literacy Achievement* (Portsmouth NH. Heinemann, 1993 a). We recommend that teachers buy this book and become familiar with the process for taking a running record. One observation survey can be done in every guided reading session by focusing on one child each time during the actual reading part of the lesson. To take a running record, the teacher uses a coding system to record the reading behavior. A separate form or piece of paper is used to record the words as they are read. A word read correctly is recorded with a checkmark. Symbols are used to record substitutions, omissions, insertions, repetitions, self-corrections, and occasions when the child is completely stuck, and is told the word. The teacher does not intervene but simply records what the child reads. This process gives a snapshot of what the child is able to do without adult support. The technique provides a rich collection of data and can be used to show progress over time. **There is no way to collect richer data about children's reading progress and needs, than to use Running Records.**

## Guided Reading Lessons and Lesson Plans

The following outline contains the elements that we include in a guided reading session. Each session is approximately thirty minutes long and follows the same basic structure. We sometimes vary the length of the different components of the lesson, taking our cues from the children's responses and needs, as well as from the books themselves. Therefore, the sessions are not bound by a fixed time frame. Where possible we try to link each reading session to a concrete experience that will build vocabulary. The following pages provide a general outline and criteria for conducting and assessing a Guided Reading Lesson. A generic Guided Reading Lesson Plan is on page 77. Next, we move to the more specific and discuss the skills and reading behaviors for beginning readers, developing readers, and fluent young readers. A sample Guided Reading Lesson and an accompanying sample Guided Reading Lesson Plan for a specific book are included for all three groups.

*Reading With Beginning Readers*

These children are the most inexperienced readers and may need to understand, learn, and practise the following reading behaviors:

- print directionality from right to left;
- the return sweep at the end of a line;
- the use of picture clues to predict words;
- one-to-one correspondence of one spoken word to one word written on the page;
- phonemic awareness: the matching of spoken sounds to written symbols;
- reading the punctuation and noticing how it sounds;

| GUIDED READING LESSON PLAN |
| --- |

**OBJECTS OR CONCRETE EXPERIENCES:**
- Choose a small collection of objects to build anticipation, or to help the children to make predictions.
- Identify a related experience that could take place before or after the reading.

**1. INTRODUCE THE BOOK**
- Talk about the book generally:
– Name the title and author.
– Give a brief outline of what it is about.
– Look at front and back covers.

**2. TALK ABOUT THE BOOK**
- Turn the pages and talk about the pictures.
- Look for suprises.
- Skim the text and point out important features.
- Predict what will happen.
- Relate the book to the children's own experience, and bring out prior knowledge.
- Show objects to help children anticipate the text.
- Build anticipation for the reading to come.

**3. VOCABULARY/SKILL**
- Locate and explain specific vocabulary that may offer challenges.
- Determine what strategy or skill may be effectively introduced.

**4. READING**
- This can be as a group, with partners, individually, aloud, or silently.
- The teacher may read certain sections of the text.

**6. RESPONDING**
- Going beyond the reading:
– Retell what the text was about.
– Relate the text to other stories or to children's own experience.
– Reflect on the meaning of the text. What questions does it raise? What meanings can we find?

**7. EXTENDING**
- Developing ideas beyond the story.
- Suggestions for further activities in writing, art, construction, etc.

**8. READ ALOUD CONNECTION**
- Suggestions for other books that could be read aloud by the teacher to the class.

- location of title and the author's and illustrator's names on the cover and title page;
- sight recognition of frequently encountered words; and
- recognition of initial consonants.

## Sample Guided Reading Lesson For Beginning Readers

### Reread a known book.

You may wish to start the lesson by going over the book you read last time. Have the children read it on their own each in their own time. Use this time to observe one child and record the information.

### Introduce the new book and talk through it.

Talk about the pictures. Turn all the pages and look for suprises. Relate the book to the children's own experiences. Perhaps use some objects to stimulate interest. Discuss what happens in the story and explain vocabulary that occurs. Cue the reader by phrasing questions which highlight specific text. For example, in *Four Black Puppies* ask, "How many *puppies* are there?"

### Vocabulary and Skill Focus.

Locate individual items of vocabulary that may be challenging. Reinforce the learning of high frequency words. Notice beginning consonants. Refer to letters in children's own names. Locate repeated words and patterns. Use your finger to show directionality of print.

### Children read the book on their own, at their own pace.

Observe each child as they read. Notice their finger pointing, places where they hesitate, or where there are problem areas in the text. Teach fix-up strategies.

### Talk about the story.

Ask children to retell it in their own words. Relate it to other stories or to familiar events. Reflect on the meaning of the story. Ask, "What did it make you think about? What do you wonder or question?"

*Sample Guided Reading Lesson Plan for Beginning Readers*

| |
|---|
| GUIDED READING LESSON PLAN FOR BEGINNING READERS<br>*Peter's Painting* by Sally Moss, illustrated by Meredith Thomas.<br>Mondo Publishing, 1995. |
| OBJECTS OR CONCRETE EXPERIENCES<br>• picture frame; paintbrush; paintbox or tubes of paint; |
| 1. INTRODUCE THE BOOK<br>• Read the title and the back of the book, *"Peter's Painting* by Sally Moss. This is a story about a boy who loves to paint." |
| 2. TALK ABOUT THE BOOK<br>• Turn the pages and talk about the pictures. "I wonder what he will paint? What would you paint if you could paint a beautiful picture?" Show the pictures. "As Peter painted over and over some magic happened. The more he painted, the more real things became." |
| 3. VOCABULARY/SKILL<br>• Past tense verbs are important in this story. Locate and read: flew, slithered, swam, twinkled, leaped, painted. Note the **ed** endings for most of the past tense verbs.<br>• This book works in a special way. It has black text on white pages, then white text on colored pages. The colored pages occur when Peter's paintings come to life. |
| 4. READING<br>• All read together the first time through, out loud.<br>• Reread by yourself in your own time.<br>• Observe one child reading and make notes, or do a Running Record. |
| 5. RESPONDING<br>• Going beyond the reading:<br>– Retell what happened in order. What did he paint?<br>– Relate the story to students' experience. What have you painted? What do you like to paint?<br>– Reflect on the story. What would happen if your paintings came to life? What will Peter paint next? |
| 6. EXTENDING<br>• Make an art gallery in your classroom.<br>– Label everyone's picture (e.g., "Maxine's Painting").<br>– Label everyone's painting with action words (e.g., "Maxine's dog jumped and jumped and jumped.").<br>– Ask the students, "Do we know an artist we can talk to? Is there an art gallery we can visit?" |
| 8. READ ALOUD CONNECTION<br>*The Incredible Painting of Felix Clousseau* by Jon Agee<br>*All I See* by Cynthia Rylant |

*Suggest activities that could be done as follow-up to the story.*

These can include making their own version of the story; painting a picture; illustrating with modelling clay; acting out the story with puppets; and using magnetic letters or chalkboards to practise a new word learned in the story, etc.

## Reading With Developing Readers

Developing readers are beginning to use strategies successfully when they encounter new words. They tend to read word-by-word quite slowly. Developing confidence and fluency is the focus for instruction. In the guided reading session they need to learn and practise the following behaviors:

- using pictures to predict what a word means or what will come next;
- using meaning cues to predict events;
- using knowledge of "what makes sense" in a sentence (structural cues);
- using the initial consonant, consonant blend, or digraph to unlock a new word;
- reading with phrasing and expression;
- noticing punctuation to assist expression and fluency;
- using language patterns, rhymes, and repetitions with confidence;
- noticing and using familiar patterns in words to unlock new words (I know *rain* so I can also read *train*); and
- retelling ideas and events from the text in a way that shows understanding.

## Sample Guided Reading Lesson For Developing Readers

*Reread a book that the group has worked with previously.*

Children read independently at their own pace. Use this time to carry out an observation or Running Record with one child.

*Introduce the new book.*

Talk about the pictures. Turn all the pages and look for suprises. Relate the book to the children's own experiences. Use objects to encourage

| GUIDED READING LESSON PLAN<br>*Arthur's Chicken Pox* by Marc Brown. Little, Brown & Co., 1994. |
|---|
| OBJECTS OR CONCRETE EXPERIENCES:<br>thermometer; coughdrops; crazy straw; circus tickets or poster; balloon; marker pen; baby powder. |
| 1. INTRODUCE THE BOOK<br>• Read the title, "*Arthur's Chicken Pox* by Marc Brown." Review the back cover and read the other titles in the series. Share the titles that children may have read before.<br>• Read the Dedication to the "chicken pox experts" and ask if there are any chicken pox experts in the group. |
| 2. TALK ABOUT THE BOOK<br>• Turn the pages and talk about the pictures.<br>• Use the objects to build anticipation.<br>• Introduce the characters, Arthur and his sister D.W. |
| 3. VOCABULARY/SKILL<br>• Locate and explain vocabulary essential to the meaning that may offer challenges: trapeze, faking/pretending, treats, soothing, allowed, disappointed, moaning, torturing.<br>• This is one book in a series. The author tells lots of stories about Arthur and D.W. Discuss how the characters stay the same, and relate to each other in the same ways each time. |
| 4. READING<br>• This can be as a group, in partners, individually, aloud, or silently. The teacher may read certain sections of the text. Choose the best way for your purposes.<br>• Observe one child reading and make notes or do a Running Record. |
| 5. RESPONDING<br>• Going beyond the reading:<br>– Retell what the text was about<br>– Relate the text to other stories or to children's own experience<br>– Reflect on the meaning of the text. What questions does it raise? |
| 6. EXTENDING<br>• Suggestions for further activities in writing and art include writing a sequel, "D.W.'s Chicken Pox," or writing the story of their own chicken pox.<br>• Extensions in science include using thermometer to experiment with different substances: hot and cold water, soil, sand, ice cubes, etc. |
| 7. READ ALOUD<br>*Sick* by Shel Silverstein |

predictions about the story, or to teach new words, especially to second language learners. Discuss what happens and use vocabulary that occurs. Explain word meanings where these may be problematic or new. Ask for predictions about the book. Locate high-frequency words in the text.

*Children read the book on their own, at their own pace, then altogether as a group.*

Observe each child as they read. Deal with difficulties and answer questions. Notice problems and teach fix-up strategies.

*Talk about the story.*

Ask children to retell it in their own words. Relate it to other stories or to familiar events. Reflect on the meaning of the story.

*Suggest activities that could be done as follow up to the story.*

Possible suggestions include writing a response to the book in a Reading Journal; copying new words learned into a personal dictionary; or making a mask for one of the characters to use in a play of the story.


### Reading With Fluent Independent Readers

Children who read at this level begin to self-correct and to try a variety of strategies, checking one against the other. They have a sight vocabulary that enables them to read simple texts with fluency, and they recognize phonemic patterns which they use to assist decoding. In the guided reading group, the following behaviors are practised:

- self-correcting when meaning is unclear;
- using and integrating structural, phonemic and meaning cues;
- developing fluency through attention to language patterns;
- learning new word meanings;
- questioning the story and checking meaning;
- talking about ideas from the text in ways that indicate understanding;
- making connections between texts;
- understanding and empathizing with characters' actions; and
- developing fluent phrasing in oral reading.

## Sample Guided Reading Lesson For Fluent Independent Readers

*Introduce a new book or review the book that the group is working with.*

If this is a new book, build prior knowledge by discussing key concepts. If this is a continuation go over the story so far. Ask for predictions about the coming section. Remind the group about some key vocabulary and ideas in the book.

*Give students time to read silently.*

Use this time to do an observation or Running Record of one or more children.

*Review the section.*

Talk about the story. Ask children to retell it in their own words. Relate it to other stories or to familiar events. Ask the children to locate certain information. Find important words. Ask them to discuss what they have read and to reflect on the main issues. Were there any problems? Was there anything anyone didn't understand? Did this reading answer questions they had raised before? Were predictions confirmed?

*Ask volunteers to read a paragraph out loud.*

Ask them to choose a part they liked and say why they liked it. Listen for fluency and reading with understanding.

*Suggest activities that could be done as follow-up to the story.*

Some suggestions include writing a response to the book in a Reading Journal; copying new words learned into a personal dictionary; working on a character sketch for one of the characters, adding new information learned in this section.

*Record the reading.*

Have the students keep a record of the pages read on a record sheet.

*Suggest further reading.*

Talk with the group about other reading they are doing. Connect this book to others in the collection.

*Sample Guided Reading Lesson For Fluent Independent Readers*

| GUIDED READING LESSON PLAN<br>*Allen Jay and the Underground Railroad* by Marlene Targ Brill |
|---|
| OBJECTS OR CONCRETE EXPERIENCE:<br>• peas in the pod; cornbread; prayer book; cloth napkin; corn cob on stalk; basket; and fishing pole |
| 1. INTRODUCE THE BOOK<br>• This book, *Allen Jay and the Underground Railroad*, is about a time in history when people were kept as slaves. Many of them ran away from their masters to seek freedom.<br>• Look for the summary statement on the copyright page and read it.<br>• Read the back and front cover of the book. |
| 2. TALK ABOUT THE BOOK<br>• Turn the pages and talk about the pictures.<br>• Skim the text and point out that this is written in the form of a diary. It is an historical memoir, an account of something that happened from the point of view of the boy.<br>• Relate the book to the children's own experience and bring out prior knowledge.<br>• Discuss the major concepts of slavery and freedom. Briefly discuss the Quaker religion.<br>• Show objects to help children anticipate the text. Build anticipation for the reading to come. |
| 3. VOCABULARY/SKILL<br>• Locate and explain specific vocabulary that may offer challenges "thee" (used for "thou" throughout) starched; runaway; scarred with whip burns; falsehoods; cautioned; vowed.<br>• Discuss the form of the language. It reflects the way English was spoken at that time. |
| 4. READING<br>• Guide the children through a reading of the author's note out loud together. Clarify understanding if needed. Then choose one of the following means of reading the story: as a group, in partners, individually aloud or silently. |
| ·5. RESPONDING<br>• Going beyond the reading:<br>– Retell what the text was about.<br>– Relate the text to other stories or to children's own experience.<br>– Reflect on the meaning of the text. What questions does it raise? What meanings can we find? |
| 6. EXTENDING<br>• Developing ideas beyond the story. Suggestions for further activities in writing, art, drama, include writing their own stories about a runaway; simple weaving to make a basket (teacher-assisted); and creating a "still scene" from the book. |
| 7. READ ALOUD<br>*Drinking Gourd* by F.N. Monjo<br>*Aunt Harriet's Underground Railroad* by Faith Ringgold |

*BLACKLINE MASTER FOR TEACHERS TO DEVELOP THEIR OWN GUIDED READING LESSON PLANS*

| GUIDED READING LESSON PLAN |
|---|
| 1. INTRODUCE THE BOOK |
| 2. TALK ABOUT THE BOOK |
| 3. VOCABULARY/SKILL |
| 4. READING |
| 5. RESPONDING<br>• Retell<br>• Relate<br>• Reflect |
| 6. EXTENDING |
| 7. READ ALOUD |

## The Reading Conference

The teacher's listening and sharing time is of course severely rationed because of the number of children in the class. While we share books with individual children the rest of the class must be busy with other tasks that do not need our constant intervention, such as writing, creating, building, or sharing a book with a friend.

In guided reading groups we choose the book and we structure the lesson to make sure that certain specific skills are addressed. In individual conferences we prefer to let the child select the book, and we then adapt the way we respond to the reading, depending on the book and the reader's developmental level. We might want to make a suggestion for a title, but if a child is interested in a book, the task of reading to an adult is not only less threatening but also more successful and hence enjoyable. Therefore, we often begin this special sharing time with the statement, "Find a book that you would like to share with me." How we share the book they choose changes, of course, from one child to the next. We modify our instructional listening and sharing to suit each individual child's level of reading skill. Children read books in a number of ways. Each requires different responses from the professional listener.

When we are sharing a book with a child, we use their *reading log* to record our observations about their knowledge of print. The reading log is a scribbler or notebook ruled up in three columns.

This is Peter's seventh reading log, from February of his Grade 1 year.

There is space to record the title and the date of the reading. There is also space for a comment. This log is a record of everything Peter reads in the classroom.

In the first entry he filled in the title and the date of reading by himself. Linda used the comment section to note that he has retold the story with gusto and total accuracy. She also wrote a note for me to suggest to his buddy reader that they share the same pattern book *Have You Seen My Duckling?* by Nancy Tafuri at their next visit.

The next entry was done independently by Peter after one of his frequent visits to the library corner. He carefully filled in the comment section with a happy face to tell us he liked the book. The third entry is again a record of a reading time that Peter and Linda spent together. She used the comment section to note that during this time she read some of the text and Peter filled in where he could.

This log is a very important record-keeping device. It allows the teacher to keep track of what the child is reading and how often he is reading with the teacher. It allows her to suggest further independent reading material to him. Linda recommends Anthony Browne's *Things I Like* to Peter and suggests he read it during the next work period time. When teachers follow up on these suggestions, the children are more eager to extend their reading selections and to venture into new territory!

This personal reading log is also used by Peter himself to record what he has read independently during the individual or book-corner reading time. This information is very valuable to Linda in reading conferences with Peter. She can see if Peter has read a particular story before, if it is one of a series of stories that he enjoys, or if it is a first-time read. This information helps Linda modify her responses so that the help she offers is of the utmost value.

In the following scenarios we offer some suggestions about the form that an individual reading conference might take.

### Reading With Beginning Readers

#### Timothy

Timothy is a lively four-year-old who loves to pore over books. He spends many profitable hours in the library corner with his friends and stuffed animals reading from memory his favorite tales and poems. He delights in the pictures, the rhythm of the language, and his ability to entertain. He often brings his favorite book, **Mr. Magnolia**, to read to me. For children such as Timothy, who are at this stage, a reading session is simply a matter of having an adult listen to them retell an often-heard story and confirm their skill at this task. Children who read in this manner often select old favorites such as **Each Peach Pear Plum**; **Rosie's Walk; Where the Wild Things Are**; and **Jillian Jiggs.** For these children we spend our instructional time talking about their choice of book and sharing the humor, pathos, or information that this book offers. We draw the children's attention to the pictures and encourage them to extend the text of the story using the information found in the illustrations. Toward the end of the session we might read a short pattern or concept book that we think the child could easily begin to read independently, inviting them to notice the print on the page. With Timothy I read books such as **What a Tale, Where's Spot?,** and **Home Sweet Home. Where's Spot?** was our all-time favorite as Timothy tried to guess what was under each flap. We close this time together by helping Timothy and children like him to fill in their reading log with the titles of the books we have shared.

*Yusef*

When Yusef brings me the pattern book **Cat on the Mat** by Brian Wildsmith, my responses are different from those I give to Timothy when he is simply retelling a favorite story. Yusef is already familiar with this book and is keen to practise his reading skill. All I need to do is set the initial pattern and Yusef is successfully and proudly able to complete the story. I begin the reading with "The cat sat on the . . ." and pause on the word "mat." I wait for Yusef to guess. He immediately fills in with the word "mat." Then together we examine the next page and try to guess who will sit on the mat next. Yusef looks carefully at the pictures and identifies the picture of the dog. He reads with me, "The dog sat on the mat. . ." Now he has the pattern and remembers that the pictures will clue him to the print. Together we turn the pages, examine the pictures, and predict the text, and *he* finishes the reading independently. With beginning readers such as Yusef, we consciously teach the strategy of using picture and contextual clues to make logical predictions about the words. We continually stress that print holds meaning. We introduce these readers to books from the category "First Steps." Some special favorites are John Burningham's *The Snow, The School,* and *The Dog* (among others); Jeanne Titherington's *Pumpkin, Pumpkin;* and some of the Shigeo Watanabe books such as *How Do I Eat It?* and *Hello How Are You?*

### Gus

Sometimes a beginning reader like six-year-old Gus brings a book such as *Coco Can't Wait* that is slightly too hard for him to read independently. When he immediately begins to stumble on the beginning words "Coco lives on the top of the hill," we know that a different response is required. We must do more of the reading. We begin the text, "Coco lives on the top of the . . . " and pause at the word "hill." We usually pause on a noun or an action word to encourage Gus to carry on the reading. Then we pick up the text at "in the" and "with the." We read only what he cannot read — usually the function words. Remember these little function words are largely redundant to the meaning.

We must decide when to pick up the reading. How long is too long to wait? A successful strategy is to give a silent count of five before telling the reader the troublesome word or group of words. We correct the child's own reading only if it alters the meaning of the text drastically. In *Coco Can't Wait*, Gus substitutes "grandmother" for "grandma." We make no comment about this kind of error.

On completion of this sharing time, we usually suggest simple pattern books that these readers can read independently with a friend, a parent volunteer, their reading buddy, or with their parents and/or siblings at home. A good suggestion is the Brian Wildsmith book, *What a Tale*, or his "First Steps" book, *The Island*. We record these suggestions along with the stories we have shared in the child's personal reading log.

This is an exciting stage for both of us as the child's progress is often rapid. Gus moved from reading very simple pattern books to "First Steps" books in a matter of weeks. As he gained skill through practice and repeated success, less and less help was required from me. We have found that, at this particular stage of reading development, teachers are the child's best listeners because of our skill in knowing when to pause, when to fill in words, and when to correct the child's efforts. Thus we try, if possible, to see these children every day for a few minutes to read, read, read.

### Reading With Developing Readers

#### Alyssa

When Alyssa comes to read with me, I know from other reading sessions that she can read with word-to-sound correspondence. She reads the print rather than the pictures. Two areas of difficulty that readers like Alyssa encounter are stopping when they meet an unfamiliar word, or reading a word inaccurately and changing the meaning of the sentence. When Alyssa stops on the word "tucked" in Maria Polushkin's story *Mother, Mother I Want Another*, and looks to me for help, I suggest she leave out the problem word and keep on reading. When she finishes the page we go back to figure out the word. She is able to use the semantic cuing system to do this. There are a number of other strategies that we use to get children like moving forward again. We suggest that the reader:

- Start again and reread the sentence. Say, "Go back and read it again."
- Consider possible meanings for the word. Say, "What makes sense here?" or "What would sound right?"
- Look at the first letter. Say, "What sound does that make? Maybe that will give you a clue."

While we are deliberately teaching the children to use semantic, syntactic, and phonic cues we do not belabor this. As soon as the mechanical process of reading starts taking over the joy, the desire to read is lost.

When Alyssa reads a harder book for her, Thacher Hurd's *Mama Don't Allow*, and miscues "The Swamp Band played far into the lake" instead of "The Swamp Band played far into the night," she has changed the meaning of the story. I stop her and ask if what she read made sense to her. When she replies, "Not really," I direct her to reread the sentence and look carefully at the last word. She immediately says, "That isn't right. It doesn't start like lake." With some help from me she is able to figure out that the word is "night" not "lake."

When I now ask her if this makes sense, she says, "Of course, it starts and ends right. . . ."

When children read a word inaccurately and change the meaning, we must continually pose the question, "Does that make sense to you?" If the children respond in the negative or seem unsure, we tell them to make another guess until the text makes sense to them. If their miscues or errors make sense, we do not correct them. But at the end of the reading time we may go back and examine some of these words. At this point we suggest that the children use their knowledge of phonics to make another guess. We are very selective about this technique; if overused, it can undermine the fragile confidence of the children.

At the end of the sharing time, we ask the children to fill in their reading logs, and we take the opportunity to suggest other texts they could read independently. I suggest to Alyssa, who seems to like funny books, that she read Peter Goodspeed's *A Rhinoceros Wakes Me Up In The Morning*. The books we might suggest are from the categories "Step A Little Further" and "Step a Little Faster." We also try to link these suggestions to current classroom interests. I suggest to Alyssa that she read *The Last Puppy* by Frank Asch, as the class has just begun a unit on pets.

### Reading With Fluent Independent Readers

#### Jeremy

When we listen to children who read fluently, self-correct their errors, and understand the author's meaning, we know that the battle of cracking the code has been won! It is no longer necessary to hear them read every word of the story. They are able to decode the text by themselves, but they still require our help to probe the deeper meanings of the story. After Jeremy read Charlotte Zolotov's *My Grandson Lew*, he and I shared together the pain of the death of our grandfathers. Jeremy remembered how his grandfather, even when he was sick, played card games with him. I told him about the mock World War I battles, complete with horses and riders, that my grandfather and I used to enact in my grandmother's back vegetable patch. We both cried. I gave him Susan Varley's *Badger's Parting Gifts* and told him that it had made me feel a little better about death. After reading the book he said, "It's a good book but not as good as *Wilfred Gordon McDonald Partridge*. It helps you think of really good memories."

It is with newly fluent children like Jeremy that we use a *reading response journal*. We want to establish a dialogue between us, reader to reader, equal in our enjoyment of books. We want the children to explore the kinds of feelings that stories evoke in us as readers. A reading response journal makes the connection between reading and writing, provides us with a record of the reading conference and the books that we have shared, and gives us insights into the understandings that children have brought to their reading. We have no need to set comprehension questions, because what the children write in their journals shows us what they have understood. They, not the teacher, set the agenda. They show us what is significant for them in the story. It is our responsibility to respond to each child's ideas and to extend the learning.

Each child has a notebook in which, when they have finished reading a story independently, they record the title of the book, the date read, and a short comment. We encourage the children to write a letter to us, not retelling every detail of the story but rather expressing what feelings this story evoked and what links to their own lives were illuminated. This letter provides a starting point for our reading conference. It gives us an entrance into the children's thoughts and feelings. At the conclusion of the reading conference, we take the time to reply in letter form. We offer some glimpse into our own lives and the ways the books have touched us. We usually end our reply with a comment that requires some response from the child. In this way a dialogue is established over time. When we show this kind of interest, the children's responses are richer and more insightful.

One day Alison brought a new copy of Robin Muller's *Tatterhood* to school and I read it at read-aloud time to the class. This led to much discussion about heroines in stories. In Alison's reading response journal I pose the question, "Do you know any other books with brave girls in them?" Her reply and the written conversation that ensued over the next few days are shown on page 93.

On another occasion a class wrote to their teacher after she had read *Leo the Late Bloomer* to them. The authors thank Jane Murphy and her students in the O.M. MacKillop Public School for sharing the samples of their work (on pages 94-95).

Sharing time with children who can read is not so much a matter of

Dear Alison, I love the book you brought.
Tarreshood is very brave. Do you know
any other books with brave girls in them?

love from Ms. Wells, Sept. 16th

Dear Ms Wells I Dono Eginl That is brave
Mollie Whuppie and The Giant hen
Sisters wereshurdi Aro Mellie whuppie
Want a cross Litte Bit of hair
carning A sistr at a time
Mollie Whuppie Was brave
Very Very Brave. From Alison

Dear Alison,
Please read Do Not Ope.
Do you think Miss Moodie is brave?

love from Ms wells

Dear MS We Ells.
Miss Moodie is brave Verey Verey
Brave But She Is
Skard Of Mes.
From Alison

Alison's Reading Response Journal

Dear
Jennifer,
I'm sure
your aunt
was very
worried.
Does your
cousin talk
a lot now?
The story
reminded
of how I
worry about
children who
that have trouble reading and writing

May 22, 1990.

Leo The Late Bloomer

ramis. mas me of my.

MOMtooD my of wanM/.

casin Dinit tok intiL.

She wsas Thee yer oD

MrS M. Wat DasThesor maDyouDR I worry too

---

May 22, 1990.
Leo the late Bloomer
It remind'd me of
wan I didn- now how
to spael and than a
few minit lader I spield
a weroo finle.

May 22, 1990    Carmen

Leo the Late Bloomer

The book about Leo the Late Bloomer

It rimend me of when I was a baby

my mom woried about me becuse I

had no hair. But now I have

hair

---

May 22, 1990  Leo
The Late Bloomer
IT reMiNed Me of
WAN I CONe der
reNde ANd riT
PViN ON PAr BAOT
IC d SAI A WeNd

listening to them as they practise decoding, but more a matter of helping them respond to the stories to deepen their comprehension.

It has also been our experience that young fluent readers, like their adult counterparts, read books that require varying degrees of reading skills.

Seven-year-old Robert is a fluent reader in Grade 1. His reading log shows that he read an old favorite, *Fix-It*, one day, began the First Novel, *Flat Stanley* the next day; and then turned to a McDonald Starter's book on *Snakes*.

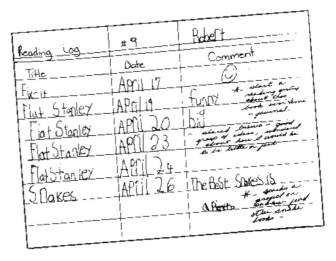

Interest, availability, peer recommendations, and the mood of the time all play a part in what the children select to read, just as they do for adults. We encourage this way of selecting reading materials and only intervene when the children seem to be in a reading rut, afraid to branch out into new and different genres. The record of titles read is of great importance because it gives us information about what the children have been reading and if it is necessary to intervene in their choices.

We use many different strategies to lure these readers toward new and more challenging texts.

- We read a book to the class and then suggest the child read another book by the same author.
- We keep a collection of books that the children have recommended as "must reads" on permanent display in the classroom.
- We regularly collect books by one special author, research the author's background, and make a display to be shared by the whole class. We can direct hesitant readers to this collection.
- As part of our theme centre, we always have many different books

at different levels of difficulty to be pored over by the children. We might suggest that a child who is in a reading rut research the theme, using the books available as a starting point.

This approach to teaching reading allows us to work with children with widely different reading abilities who are interested in the same book. Literature, unlike some basals, lends itself beautifully to use by children with different reading skills. A book such as *Mr. Gumpy's Outing* can be retold by Timothy, partially read by Gus, and fluently enjoyed by Alyssa. It is up to us as professional listeners to modify our responses so that each of these readings is both successful and productive for the child.

For Timothy, who retells me an old favorite, I enjoy the rendition, praise his skill, laugh with him at the pictures, and ask him to tell me who he thinks made the boat tip. He looks at me with concentration and says, "I don't think it was any one of them, it was them all. What do you think?" Talk is generated by this reading and our time is spent sharing our ideas. Gus needs me to share the reading with him. My role is to put in the function words and any other vocabulary that he finds difficult so that the flow of the reading is not inhibited or interrupted. Alyssa fluently decodes the text, self-corrects her errors, and understands the author's meaning. However, she tires before the ending of the book and I finish the reading. Alison reads this book from beginning to end by herself. She requires a response from me that will deepen her understanding of the text and help her to place this story into the context of her own life. I ask her to think what she would do if she was tipped out of a boat. She responds very quickly, "I'll be okay, I always wear a life jacket. I have a boat and a cottage. I know all about boats, my dad and mom taught me." The more we work with real books, the more we realize how these books can serve a variety of purposes for different readers.

Teachers often ask us, "But how do you know what kind of responses to make to children? How do you know when to take over the reading? How do you know when to correct?" The answer to all these is quite simple. LISTEN TO THE CHILD READ, TAKE INTO ACCOUNT THE CHILD'S STAGE OF READING DEVELOPMENT, AND THEN USE YOUR OWN COMMON SENSE. Remember to view errors not as dreadful mistakes but as windows to more effective instruction. Listening to children is the key component of our language program.

It is also important to EXAMINE THE CHILDREN'S' WRITING.

Children such as Zhu who are still experimenting with letters and sounds and have not yet established a clear sound-letter understanding are usually at the memorization stage of the reading process. They are still beginning readers.

ABOCHLRERi
SSOSCCoPPomm

Anna has the beginnings of an understanding of how words are constructed and represents words with one or more dominant sounds. Remember, children like Anna can usually read, with a little pattern-setting by the teacher, simple pattern and "First Steps" books. These are the beginning readers.

IVMIME

Joel's emerging skill in composition is shown by his use of spaces, conventional spellings for the more common function words (is, and, the) and by his ability to identify correctly, for the most part, the dominant sounds in individual words.

```
Irie  SAHePs   CLAHrA  sces  The  wruo,  AT
'TWJ  is The SAHeP  CLABEA"
HesTin THe PeoPal  CAHO  THe      SAHePs  CUABEA
ANe it  Le'ih ForiADa
```

As a developing reader, Joel can read books at the levels of "Step a Little Further" and "Step a Little Faster." Children like Joel require a shared reading experience in which you read those passages that are too difficult for them to manage alone. They are usually past the memorization stage, read pattern book easily, and are now ready to tackle, with some adult aid, books such as *The New Baby Calf*. Children's reading and writing develop in tandem, and our analysis of their written work helps us to coach their reading appropriately.

# FIVE

# Making the Most of Space and Time

## Active Learning Centres

"How do I organize space and time in the classroom and keep track of the children's activities?" is a question many primary grade teachers ask themselves. It often seems difficult to maximize the time teachers and children have to spend on reading and writing activities. What are all the other children doing while the teacher is holding personal, shared, or guided reading and writing conferences? In this chapter we look at the physical organization of the room, the routines that the children follow, the storage and display of the books, the way the teacher allocates time, and how the teacher tracks the children's activities. These are all critical components of any successful literacy program.

The first decision that teachers need to make is how to organize the school day. The program that we describe needs large blocks of time so that the children can pursue in depth a wide variety of activities related to literacy.

Picture the following Grade 1/2 classroom during the work period. Some children are independently illustrating a book they have just produced, others are involved with a challenge card in the sand, others are listening to a favorite tape, others are sharing a book with a friend, and still others are productively occupied with an open-ended mathematical challenge. Two girls have built a medieval castle using the large blocks and are writing invitations to knights to come to a tournament. At the art centre, four children are constructing a dragon from boxes and tissue paper that will hang from the ceiling. Two boys are sewing pillows in the shape of dragons. The teacher is sitting at a round table sharing a book with a child, while several other children are working at the table on their reading journals and their latest piece of writing. This is the classroom at work, not for half an hour during "centre" time but for most of the day! This scene can be found in any classroom where there are four-, five-, six-, seven-, and eight-year-olds who are actively engaged in their learning. The only variation is, that as the age of the children increases, the complexity of their work also increases.

The secret to the creation of such a focused and productive learning environment is the stimulus that comes from the books that we read and the topics we discuss. The organization allows for large blocks of time for the children to become actively engaged in a wide variety of meaningful tasks, working in well-equipped and organized learning centres where materials can be found and used. Success depends upon our creating opportunities for the children to direct and select their own activities and learning objectives, establishing clear expectations for student behavior, and setting up simple, manageable routines. Children become highly motivated to learn when the activities are self-selected and genuinely interesting to them.

### Learning Centres

If our students are truly going to be given the opportunity to explore topics that interest them and to engage in tasks that will stimulate them to reflect, question, discuss, write, read, and seek new answers and understandings, we believe the presence of permanent learning centres in our classrooms is vital. Teachers have long understood that for any active learning program to run smoothly, the children must have easy, independent access not only to these permanent centres but also to any supplies that they might require to complete their projects. The teacher can't be sharing a book with a child and finding glue at the same time.

In our program we have established several such centres, complete with detailed but simple rules for use. Each centre has a labelled space for each article to make tidy-up easy. Monitors in the older grades can be responsible for checking that the supplies are replenished at the end of the day. The number of participants allowed at each centre is clearly noted by the number of chairs or by a sign.

The children well understand from frequent group discussions that before they start any new activity, they must first clean up their old work space and then discuss their new plans with us.

### Permanent Centres That We Suggest

#### A Writing/Reading Table:

• complete with pencils, paper of various sizes and weights, erasers, staplers, tagboard or light cardboard for book covers, markers, colored pencils, rulers, and as many computers as you can find to use for composing.

#### A Library Corner:

• cosy and inviting, filled with books of every kind, a record player/tape machine with earphones and tapes for quiet listening, pillows, a rug, and a rocking chair or two for easy reading, looking, and sharing. Remember to include copies of the books shared during Guided Reading Lessons.

#### A Literacy Centre:

• where children can find the materials necessary for a wide variety of literacy-related activities and games that complement the reading and writing activities which take place elsewhere in the room. Literacy Centre activities should also help to develop the skills of letter and word recognition, spelling, phonics, and printing. Ideas for activities at this centre often spring directly from books used in the guided and shared reading sessions. Examples of activities that might be housed in this centre are:

  • **Poetry:** written on cards accompanied by sentence strips and word cards for matching. Keep the pieces in resealable plastic bags. Poems should be introduced in shared reading then placed in the centre. Each poem can be copied and placed in the child's individual poetry book (use a duotang or a scrapbook) for the children to practise reading on their own or at home.

- **Build a Poem**: on small individual cards, the teacher prepares a set of approximately 100 high frequency words (nouns, verbs, adjectives and adverbs, prepositions, conjunctions, and pronouns). Glue a piece of magnetic strip to the back of each card and provide a cookie sheet. The children choose words and arrange them on the sheet. They then copy and illustrate their poems. An alternative way to do this activity is to copy a sheet of words for the children and have them cut out the words they want and paste them onto a piece of paper. In this case, provide a resealable plastic bag in which leftover or extra words may be stored.

- **Reading the Walls**: provide a pointer and a special pair of magical spectacles (no glass in them) for "reading the walls." Children take the pointer and go around the room reading signs, charts, and labels.

- **Chalkboards and word cards:** partner spelling games, in which one child challenges another to spell a word. Both children write the word on their chalkboard. Then they check its correct spelling on a list before tackling another word.

- **Magnetic Letters:** Students use the letters and a cookie sheet for making words. (*Note*: This is *in addition* to the Build a Poem activity.)

- **Letter-Sound Collections**: plastic bags or small boxes containing objects that all begin with the same sound for classification and spelling. Children can make their own little books for each sound with pictures and words in them.

- **Scrabble**™ and other commercially produced word games.

- **Word-matching:** bingo games, to teach key words and words used in themes.

- **Teacher-made Reading Games:** games which use dice and game boards, and must involve reading. Children like to be involved in making such games and often have great ideas for designing the track boards and game cards.

- **Response to Reading Activities:** for children who are reading fluently. Instructions can be printed on cards and children can choose a response idea after reading a book. Some ideas are journal writing, puppet plays, character descriptions, maps of the setting, posters advertising the book, new book jackets, and so on. Provide Plasticine™ and boards for making illustrations in response to a story they have read. These activities should be introduced to the class and the criteria for success should be discussed before they are put into the centre for choosing.

- **Listening Centre:** Complete with headsets, tapes, and books to go with them.

- **Printing activities:** designed to give practice at letter formation. Children can copy letters from cards, trace letters in sand or on sand paper, or use tracing paper.

- **Computer activities**: the computer provides a centre for word processing, in terms of both composing and publishing children's writing. There is also excellent educational software available to help develop literacy (e.g., *Wiggle Works* from Scholastic).

*A Dramatic Play Centre:*

- which, depending on the interests of the children or the supplies the teacher provides, can change from a house, to a nursery, to a store, to a restaurant, to an office, to whatever the children decide. Remember to include paper and pencils for notes, and books for interest, enjoyment, and information. Make specific suggestions about how writing and reading can be used at the centre.

*An Art Centre:*

- that houses paper of every weight and color, glue that really sticks, scissors both left- and right-handed that really cut, material and found material such as small boxes, toilet-paper rolls, egg cartons, toothpicks, cotton balls, etc. To keep this centre tidy, try keeping the paper in a puzzle tray, the glue in plastic bottles stored in a work caddy with a handle for easy carrying, and all other materials in individually labelled buckets that stack.

*A Paint Centre:*

- that changes regularly to include new colors of paint or dye and different kinds of paint materials such as squirt paint, blow paint, finger paint, and soap paint for special projects. We like to keep our paints in special covered plastic jars that sit securely in a long tray. This unit is easily available from most school art-supply companies. The children paint either on an oilcloth on the floor or at an easel. Some teachers prefer to add the paints to the art centre to encourage both multi-media work and to save on space. Whether you have one or two centres really depends on your physical space and goals.

*A Building/Construction Centre:*

- that provides a wide variety of building materials, both found materials (e.g., plastic bottles, lids, caps, buttons), and commercially produced materials (e.g., Zaks, Lego, Tinkertoy, Kapla, and blocks of every size and shape). To keep this centre manageable and quiet, store the materials in individually labelled buckets and add a carpet to deaden the noise. Add a changing inventory of props — labelled buckets full of construction toys, small cars, people, animals, planes, and dinosaurs; and fabric, paper, pencils, and markers to help shape the learning. This centre can be divided into two — a building centre and a bin-toy centre. However, by combining these centres as suggested, the children use a wider variety of materials in more sophisticated and in-depth ways. This type of organization better suits the split focus time-table that allows for a math/science/technology period every day. During this designated time all the children must work at math/science/technology activities.

*A Mathematics/Science/Technology Centre:*

- When we started, we had two centres that dealt with math/science/ technology concepts. However, we discovered that teachers find it is more practical to have one large centre because materials and activities complement and enrich each other. In this centre teachers provide a wide variety of manipulative materials for the children to use as they seek to make sense of the world of numbers, geometry, measurement, and scientific discovery. Some suggested materials are measuring tapes, wheels, scales, pattern blocks, geoboards, counters of every size, color and shape, chart paper, graph paper, and pencils.

  Magnifying glasses, scales, books, and interesting collections to examine also find a place at this centre. We have found that collections of magnets, shells, or batteries usually spark the interest of children of all ages and can become the focus of the interest or theme table. Be inventive about offering other collections for your students to explore.

These materials will of course change according to the dictates of the unit of study at the time. Don't put out everything at once or chaos is sure to reign. However, some of the equipment, such as blocks, counters, and measuring tools, is necessary on a daily basis and needs to be made easily available to the children.

*A Sand and Water Centre:*

- complete with two separate tables for the sand and water — recommended because they are such rich sources of language use and problem-solving activity. Include in this centre, as in all the other centres, changing props to encourage children to use new language, pose new questions, reflect on new learning, and offer new solutions. To make tidy-up easy, we always include a small hand-held whisk broom and dustpan for the sand and a bucket and several sponges for the water. Any additional props are stored on a table with each piece individually labelled. Small cars, people, dinosaurs, or animals are kept in individually labelled tubs.

These then are the permanent centres that we would suggest you establish in your room. The teacher's role is to ensure that these centres remain vital and exciting sources of learning. These centres, if they are to offer continual challenges to the children, must be constantly changed to reflect new class interests and to accommodate the children's developing skills.

### An Interest or Theme Learning Centre

In addition to these permanent centres, we also provide an interest or theme learning centre that acts as a resource for all the areas of study. Ideas for the themes often come from the teacher or from the interests of one or two children. Teachers need to be vigilant for an interest that can serve as the beginnings of a more comprehensive theme. Some popular interests that lend themselves to cross-disciplinary use are dinosaurs, a trip to the museum; a new pet or a baby in the family; or a favorite teddy bear or book. We change the centres as needed to meet the demands of the content curriculum prescribed by individual jurisdictions. Earth studies, physical science, and biological science all offer ideas for this centre as do social studies themes such as community or family history.

The centre houses a collection of materials related to the theme, including fiction and nonfiction books, posters, interesting objects to examine and probe, puzzles, games, math challenges, and models. The permanent centres are used to extend this centre through art, reading, writing, and building.

It is important to remember that reading and writing can occur at any of the centres in the room and should not be limited to designated areas. It is essential that the classroom offer a wide variety of changing tasks that provide opportunities to question, to discuss, to retell, to reflect, to write, to relate, and to read about subjects that interest each child.

Teachers often ask, "But how do you find *room* for all of these centres?" Our solution, adopted by many of our colleagues, is simply to get rid of the individual desks that devour our classroom space. We find the children are quite content to live without a separate desk if they have a chair at one of the individual centres they can call their own and a personal bucket to hold their own special treasures. The centres, whether they are achieved by pushing the old desks together or by scrounging low tables, become the focal point of the room; and because the sharing of resources is an integral feature of these centres, the children have the opportunity to learn this important social skill through daily practice.

## The Timetable

How do you organize the day so that these centres can be used productively and the curriculum covered? There is really no necessity to timetable centres. Most school days break down into four reasonably large blocks of time — two in the morning and two in the afternoon. Each block varies from 45 to 60 minutes, and although every situation and school is different, this is a basic schedule that gives children ample working time at any given centre. The centres provide an entirely suitable working environment for children to carry out independent study and co-operative, small-group projects.

As experienced teachers, we preferred to have all of the centres open during each work period. We were very familiar with a centres approach to learning and felt comfortable offering instruction at both language centred activities and mathematics or science activities within the same work period. For our own purpose we often designated a specific work time as either a literacy time or a math/science/technology time. This was simply a technique we used to help us focus our observations and instruction. For example, if we had designated for ourselves a work period as a math/science/technology time, then we would concentrate on observing the children as they worked with the building materials at the centres. We spent our time observing and teaching specific skills that were related to mathematics or science. We often used the interest centre to introduce specific scientific concepts such as electricity or magnets. At other work times during the day we would designate the work period a literacy work period to help us focus our instruction and conferencing on literacy activities.

The following is a Suggested Timetable where all the centres are open during the work period.

### Suggested Timetable for Half-Day Morning Kindergarten Students

| | |
|---|---|
| 8:45 to 9:15 | Entrance/Book Exchange |
| 9:15 to 9:30 | Story/Discussion |
| 9:30 to 10:15 | Work Period |
| 10:15 to 10:30 | Tidy-Up and Snack Time |
| 10:30 to 10:45 | Private Book Time |
| 10:45 to 11:00 | Story/Music/Buddy Reading |
| 11:00 to 11:30 | Outdoor Play or Work Period |
| 11:30 to 11:45 | Tidy-up |
| 11:45 | Dismissal |

### Suggested Half-Day Timetable for Afternoon Kindergarten Students

| | |
|---|---|
| 1:00 to 1:15 | Entrance/Book Exchange or Private Reading Time |
| 1:15 to 1:30 | Story/Discussion |
| 1:30 to 2:30 | Work Period |
| 2:30 to 2:45 | Snack/ Music/Story/ Buddy Reading |
| 2:45 to 3:00 | Book Exchange or Private Reading Time |
| 3:00 to 3:30 | Outdoor Play or Work Period |
| 3:30 | Dismissal |

*Suggested Timetable for Full-Day Students*

|  |  |
|---|---|
| 8:45 to 9:00 | Entrance/Book Exchange |
| 9:00 to 9:30 | Story/Discussion |
| 9:30 to 10:30 | Work Period |
| 10:30 to 10:45 | Recess |
| 10:45 to 11:00 | Story/Buddy Reading |
| 11:00 to 11:45 | Work Period |
| 11:45 | Dismissal |
| Lunch | |
| 1:00 to 1:20 | Entrance/Private Reading Time |
| 1:20 to 1:30 | Story |
| 1:30 to 2:30 | Work Period |
| 2:30 to 2:45 | Recess |
| 2:45 to 3:15 | Work Period |
| 3:15 to 3:30 | Story/Buddy Reading |

However, this timeframe may present problems for some teachers with such a variety of activities available and with children at so many different developmental levels. It can feel frustrating to be pulled in so many different directions at once. The old idea of "work" and "play" periods is not an answer to this frustration. We want to involve the children in making choices about their learning because we believe that their motivation is so much higher at this age when they feel they have some control. When teacher-directed activities precede "play," some children never get to experience the open-ended self-chosen activities because "work" takes too long.

An alternative structure is to offer two distinct work periods. One period is devoted to activities related to literacy and the arts. During this time the drawing and writing tables, the library corner, the literacy centre, the art and paints centres, and the dramatic play, and interest centres are open for use. Depending upon the age of the class and your current focus you might choose to open certain of these and keep others closed on different occasions. The expectations for activities at these centres depend upon the age of the children.

The other work period has a math/science/technology focus. The children work with building and construction materials, and at the sand, water, and math/science centres. The computer is available for use during both periods with the programs used changing.

This organization gives a more manageable focus. It enables teachers to spend time in the literacy period on guided or shared reading, followed by individual reading or writing conferences.

Sometimes teachers new to a centres approach overlook the construction, sand, and water activities in favor of reading and writing instruction. With this split focus, time is spent equally on all areas of the curriculum. Children learn to read and write. They also spend equal time learning to compute with increasing sophistication, estimate, create a pattern, collect and analyze data, and pour and measure with increasing accuracy. These concrete experiences provide the conceptual framework for more abstract mathematical and scientific thinking. With this timetable the teacher's behavior makes explicit that all learning centres are valued equally. Teachers can spend quality time in all areas of the curriculum and can be confident that the girls spend as much time building as the boys do drawing and writing.

Other important learning experiences, such as physical education, music, drama, snack time, and outdoor play, must be considered when finalizing a timetable. We suggest that these be inserted into, or between, the large working periods.

### A Suggested Split Focus Timetable for a Half-Day Morning Kindergarten Class

| | |
|---|---|
| 8:45 to 9:00 | Entrance: Home borrowing |
| 9:00 to 9:15 | Story; shared reading/writing |
| 9:15 to 10:15 | Work period: literacy/art or math/science/technology |
| 10:15 to 10:30 | Sharing time |
| 10:30 to 10:45 | Private book time or Story or Music |
| 10:45 to 11:30 | Work Period: literacy/art or math/science/technology |
| 11:30 to 11:45 | Tidy up for Dismissal at 11:45 |

### A Suggested Split Focus Timetable for a Half-Day Afternoon Kindergarten Class

| | |
|---|---|
| 12:45 to 1:00 | Entrance: Home borrowing |
| 1:00 to 1:15 | Story; shared reading/writing |
| 1:15 to 2:15 | Work period: literacy/art or math/science/technology |
| 2:15 to 2:30 | Sharing time |
| 2:30 to 2:45 | Private book time or Story or Music |
| 2:45 to 3:30 | Work Period: literacy/art or math/science/technology |
| 3:30 to 3:45 | Tidy up for Dismissal at 3:45 |

*A Suggested Split Focus Timetable for a Full-Day Program*

| | |
|---|---|
| 8:45 to 9:00 | Entrance: Home borrowing |
| 9:00 to 9:15 | Story; shared reading/writing |
| 9:15 to 10:15 | Work period: literacy/art |
| 10:15 to 10:30 | Sharing time |
| 10:30 to 10:45 | Recess |
| 10:45 to 11:30 | Private book time or Story or Music |
| 11:00 to 11:30 | Work Period: continues or gym |
| 11:30 to 11:45 | Tidy up for Dismissal at 11:45 |
| Lunch | |
| 12:45 to 1:00 | Entrance: Private reading |
| 1:00 to 1:15 | Story; shared reading/writing math/science/technology focus |
| 1:15 to 2:15 | Work period: math/science/technology |
| 2:15 to 2:30 | Sharing time |
| 2:30 to 2:45 | Recess |
| 2:45 to 3:30 | Work Period: math/science/technology Deconstruction/recording time |
| 3:15 to 3:30 | Sharing time |
| 3:30 to 3:45 | Tidy up for Dismissal at 3:45 |

## Tracking Children's Activities

With such a timetable and classroom organization, teachers need to keep track of what children are doing. There are many ways to achieve this. Some teachers of younger children simply mark off, on a class list, the choices or activities that the children initially make. They intervene in the choices only when they want to work with specific children on a particular project or when they see one activity being chosen to the exclusion of all others. Many teachers who use this method require the children to show them their work before they move on to another activity. In this way, the teacher can check on what the children have done, offer suggestions for extensions, and steer the children to an activity that the teacher wants them to try.

| Activities (first choice) am sk's. | Writing/Drawing | Crafts | Paints | Blocks/Building | Sand/Water | Library | Dramatic Play | Math | Science | Reading with Me | Big Toys/Puzzles | Interest Centre – Celebrations |
|---|---|---|---|---|---|---|---|---|---|---|---|---|
| Aileen | X | | X | | | | X X | | | | | X directed |
| Susan | | XX | | | | X | | | | directed X | X | |
| Nicole | (project) XXX | | | | | X | | | | X | | |
| Denise | | XX | X | X | X | | | | | | X | |
| Amy | XX | X | | | XX | | | X | | | | |
| Sofia | | | | | | | X | XX | X | | | X |
| Nick | | | X | X | | X | | | | | X | X |
| Tomas | X | | | XX | | | | | | X | | XX |
| John | | | | | | | | X | X | X | | |

*Week of Dec 4 → 8*

Other teachers prefer to use a tracking board. One colleague makes two tracking boards. One board is for the Literacy/Arts time and include pictures of such activities as the Reading Corner, the Drawing/Writing table, the Computer, the Listening Centre, the Dramatic Play Centre, and the Interest Centre. The other board is for the Math / Science/Technology time and includes pictures of such activities as the Sand Table, the Water Table, the Big Blocks, the Building Centre, a Puzzles Centre, a Mathematics Activities Centre, and the Computer. Each board with its activities is color-coded (e.g., red for literacy activities and blue for math/science/technology activities). Attached with a clothes pin to each picture are replica cards, one for each person allowed at the centre (e.g., four pictures of the Dramatic Play Centre are attached to the Dramatic Play Centre picture and word). To work at any centre the children select a card and, using the clothespin, attach it to their clothing. When finished, they return their card to the appropriate place. One of the advantages of this method is that the teacher can see at a glance where each child should be working. Teachers who use this method also require that the children talk with them about what they have done before moving on to another activity.

There are many variations on the tracking board method. Some teachers use library card pockets. Each centre has a library pocket with a picture or a name on it and the number of children allowed to work at the centre at any one time. To work at any centre the children put their name cards in the pocket. When they are finished one activity, before moving to the next, they must put their name card in the new activity pocket.

Some teachers in the older grades prefer their students to use a tracking log or reflection journal. The teachers make a list of what is to be accomplished, either for the day, or for the week, or for the unit of study. Some activities are "musts" while others may be choices (e.g., one reading activity each day, one writing activity each day, one mathematics or science activity each day). Timelines for completion are also included. The students record what they intend to do that day in their journal and have the teacher sign it off when it is satisfactorily completed. The advantage to this method is that the teacher can track not only what the students are doing, but also see what work they have completed and how well they have done it. In addition, students may begin to learn how to reflect on their learning and write self-evaluation comments in these journals.

SIX 🙢

# *Implementing the Reading and Writing Program in Your Classroom*

## Combining the Elements on a Day-to-Day Basis

You've set up activity centres, bought the books, and decided on the timetable. Now, what are the daily ingredients of a literature-based reading program? We have discussed how you share books with individual children, hold individual and group reading conferences and guided reading sessions, and how you make responses based on individual needs. What else is happening in the classroom?

The cornerstone is the daily sharing of books with the whole class.

### *Read Aloud*

We read aloud two to four times daily, depending on whether the children attend school half-day or full-day. Reading first thing in the morning sets a positive tone for the day, and reading last thing in the afternoon helps end on an upbeat note. What do we read? EVERYTHING THAT WE FEEL CONSTITUTES GOOD LITERATURE. We share pattern books, big books, short novels, picture books, poetry, nonfiction material, favorite tales, and, of course, the children's own writing. Why do we spend so much time reading? Well, some days it seems to be the only way to capture the attention of the group! There's nothing like the power of a story to calm an excited class. We also have critical objectives for this read-aloud time. We know that when we read aloud we have the opportunity to introduce children to wonderful stories and to hook them on the act of reading. By sharing our enthusiasm, we help to instill in them a love of books, model good reading behavior, and open up new and old areas for thought and reflection. In the read-aloud time in our classrooms, we take the opportunity to introduce the children to more difficult text that is beyond their present reading ability. One of our favorites for Grade 1 and 2 students is Roald Dahl's *The Fantastic Mr. Fox.* Kindergarten children are held spellbound by Marianna Mayer's *The Black Horse.* Read-aloud time gives children the opportunity to develop their skills in prediction and critical listening and thinking. It is a time when we can model for the children how we want them to listen to others' opinions and how to question. We encourage them to defend their responses.

This read-aloud time often precedes the children's work period, and therefore, we can take the opportunity to suggest activities that would link the story with their play, their writing, and their art. Janet and Allan Ahlberg's story *The Jolly Postman* inspired Eric, Karl, and Dinesh, a group of five-year-olds, to make a series of postcards to send when they took a voyage in their submarine, made the previous day in the block centre. Robert Munsch's *The Paper Bag Princess* sparked Dino, George, Emma, and Sophia, a group of five- and six-year-olds, to make paper bag princesses, princes who were "stuck up," and fierce dragons. This group of children eventually used their puppets to make a play for their classmates. The reading of Carol and Donald Carrick's story *Patrick's Dinosaurs* inspired Amy, Daphne, Alexander, and Josh to begin simple research projects on what actually happened to the dinosaurs. This topic eventually expanded to include endangered animals and environments.

It was also a time to suggest other titles that the children might like to read on their own or with one of their reading buddies. This was a very precious part of the day, and we *never* let it be squeezed out of our timetable.


### Individual Reading Time

Once children have heard a story read aloud they often want to read it by themselves. They also want to share books they have read during guided and shared reading lessons. Of course they find books easier to read when they meet them for a second or a third time. This individual repeated reading practice is a very important component of our language program. To facilitate this practice, we always place multiple copies of books that are used in guided or shared reading into the Reading Corner.

We schedule time each day for the children to spend privately with a book. This time could be first thing in the morning, or first thing in the afternoon. The length of time should vary with the age of the children. For a class of four- and five-year-olds this might be no more than 5 to 10 minutes, while children in Grade 3 might read for 20 minutes. In some classes the whole class sits in a large circle, while in others the children select a spot of their own choosing. All choose a book from a collection brought to the middle of the circle or room. As teachers we change this selection to reflect the changing needs of the class. We make a conscious effort to include books that addressed the interests or themes of the moment. We also make available new materials and old favorites borrowed from the school library. Reading at this time for the youngest children might simply mean looking at the pictures. We do not require these children to record their selections. Children from the beginner reading stage onward were requested to write at least one or two words from the title of the book in their reading log.

This whole-class reading time gives us the opportunity to observe, to chat with one or two children about what they were reading, and to read ourselves. In addition to this whole-class reading time, the book corner is available during the work period for further private reading for all the children to enjoy.


### Buddy Reading

As well as hearing stories read aloud by the teacher and reading to themselves, children in the kindergarten and primary grades need to share books with other people as often as possible. One of the ways of providing more of this critical listening time is to start a Buddy Reading Program. This is an interclass program that teams up more fluent and older readers with beginning readers. We find this program usually works most successfully when a number of conditions are in place.

- Limit this sharing to once a week. If you do it too often it loses its impact and disrupts other programs.
- Timetable buddy reading immediately before or after recess.
- Confine the reading locations to the library, either of the two classrooms, and the halls.
- Set a time limit of 15 minutes. Many of the children enjoy this activity so much that they will spend hours, if allowed, engaged in shared reading.
- Monitor the selection of books carefully so that the young children select books that they can read with little difficulty.
- Do not put the older children in the position of "teacher." Their role is to be an interested listener.
- Hold miniworkshops with the listeners to help them be effective. Stress that when their buddy stumbles on a word, they should tell them the word. Caution them against overcorrecting the child and suggest that if their buddy makes many errors, they simply take over the reading and tell us what happened later.
- Insist that both partners record their choice of reading material in their joint reading log.

| TITLE | READER | COMMENT |
|---|---|---|
| The boy in the drawer | Pashalia | we like the part when she turned on the cold water |
| A hippopopotamos ate the teacher | Pashalia | we liked the part when it ate the teacher |
| Jimmy's boa bounce back | Pashalia | we hole booth like the book we also thought that was funny. |
| Angry Arthur | Pashalia | when he made the earth like a giant cracking egg. |
| The story of Ferdinand | Pashalia | When Ferdinand sat in the middle of the stadium and smelt the flower. |
| Coco can't wait | Pashalia | When they past each other and didnt meet. |
| The tiny tiny woman | Pashalia | we like the part when she said take it. |
| busy nights | Katie | we liked the part when they had a party |
| I know an old lady | Katie | we liked the part when the horse swallowed |
| The bath | Katie | we liked when she was playing in the mud. |
| New blue shoes | Katie | we liked when she asked if she could trade feet. |
| The patch work cat | Katie | we liked when the milk man found her. |

117

The success of a Buddy Reading Program depends upon the collaboration of the two teachers involved and the school librarian. We find we need to talk to each other regularly, be prepared to modify the program to suit the needs of both groups of children, and constantly encourage the children to share their experiences as buddy readers with us.

In some classrooms, Buddy Writing has become a natural extension of Buddy Reading. After several readings, books such as *Rosie's Walk*, *Not Now Bernard*, and *Coco Can't Wait* are natural books for simple retellings. Our youngest children could retell the story in their own words while the more sophisticated readers and writers took on the role of scribes. Together they decided on the page breaks and illustrations. These books were put with the original texts in clear resealable plastic bags for other readers to enjoy. Other books such as *Polar Bear Polar Bear, What do You Hear?* and *Somewhere* are successful jump-off books. Together the children create their own stories based on the patterns in these books. We encourage the children to use familiar names and words in their creations so that other children in the class could have success with the reading. Thus, *Brown Bear, Brown Bear, What Do You See?* easily became *Callum, Callum, What Do You See?* These classroom publications are also put with the original story so that children could make connections as they were reading.

### Home Borrowing

Another way to immerse children in stories is to start a Home Borrowing Program. This is an out-of-school reading program in which the children share books with their families. Books are borrowed on a regular basis and the children and members of their families or friends read together.

To begin:

- Make a special bag for each child. Bags can be constructed out of waterproof oil cloth with a shoulder strap and a Velcro fastener at the top to keep out the rain and the snow. The results are worth the trouble; these special bags not only give this program status but also make it easy to identify the children's bookbags. This can really help a busy family in the morning.
- Include a comment booklet that has space to record the title of the

book to be shared, the name of the reader, and comments from both the reader and the listener. Comments might include how the sharing went, whether they enjoyed the reading, and what other books they might like. Encourage family members to respond in the language that is the most comfortable for them. (There are usually older children in the school who are eager to translate these comments for us.)

> But may be I didn't give it my full concentration. The story is sterile, flat: it has no soul." Jane
>
> "Right on!

| Title | Reader | Comment |
|---|---|---|
| The Lady and the Unicorn | | I haven't read this. The illustrations are quite rich. The story is quite simple, but it's a nice enough fairy tale. The illustrations really are beautiful. |

| Title | Reader | Comment |
|---|---|---|
| Feeding Babies | | I haven't read either of these books. How are they? Emma liked the elephants best. I liked the hippos. It's a sweet book |
| Little Witch's Big Night | | E. loves stories about witches. In this book, a few kids get to have a ride on a broomstick. Loads fun! |
| Buggy Riddles | | Do you like silly riddles? I knew Emma does. She enjoyed this book even tho she didn't get many of the jokes - I like silly riddles too, even Emma's. |
| Carousel | | Wildsmith is an amazing artist! We all loved this book. |

- Try to respond to comments so that a communication channel between home and school can be opened. Again, the older, bilingual children willingly translate our comments into the languages of the homes of our students.
- Do regular inservice sessions with parents to ensure that they understand the purposes of the program. They are to listen to the child's reading in a positive manner, not overcorrecting and not afraid to take up the reading if the book is too difficult for the child. Also hold miniworkshops both for parents and older students about

how to read effectively, how to question, and how to select the books to be shared.

- Monitor the books. As with the senior buddy readers, we do not want these listeners put in the position of being the teacher.
- Home reading programs have many unexpected bonuses. Children see their parents and their teacher working together on something that both feel is important. Reading is seen to be valued both at home and at school.

Our programs help us to provide time for our students to read individually to more fluent readers. They also have another important use. They offer a ready-made opportunity for children to listen to stories on an individual basis. We use these programs to provide the time that all children require if they are to develop a love of stories and to experience the necessary number of hours spent engaged with books that precedes independent reading. Thus we encourage our school and home buddies to alternate this sharing time so that our students can take on the role both of listener and reader.

In homes where English is not read, we encourage the children to tell their parents the story and talk about the pictures in their first language. We encouraged them to read very simple, familiar pattern books. We also provide bilingual books because we want our students to hear stories in a language with which the reader feels at ease. We want this to be an enjoyable time, not a test of endurance. For this reason, we also include books and tapes, as we recognize, that in some homes there are no readers available. Parents thank us for the book and tape sets as it provides an opportunity for all their children, younger siblings included, to listen to stories.

We have expanded the idea of a home-borrowing program. In addition to stories, first language materials, and books and tapes, we now include simple homework kits. These kits consist of either the original story and a class-made sequel, or a story and accompanying vocabulary game. *Where's Spot?*, *Peepo!*, and *The Jolly Postman* are examples of books that our children eagerly turned into classroom books for home borrowing. The games are simple, derived from the vocabulary of the story. Stories such as *Where the Wild Things Are, The Paper Bag Princess* and *Whose Mouse Are You?* lend themselves to chase games. Books with less vocabulary, such as *How Do I Eat It?, The Frog and The Fly,* and *Mine's The Best,* are better suited to Bingo, Tic Tac Toe, or

Snakes and Ladders formats. Each kit is kept in a resealable plastic bag. Any instructions that are needed to play the game successfully are included in English and all the major languages of the classroom. We have a generic set of instructions for these games that we reproduce and include as needed in the various kits. Some kits are made by the children, as follow-up activities to a guided reading session, a shared reading session, or an individual reading or writing conference. Other kits are made during buddy reading or writing times. These home-work kits have proven to be very popular with both parents and children as they seem to better answer the cry from parents for "real" homework.

Our home borrowing programs have been very successful and have helped to turn our classrooms into environments where books literally take over. Children can't get enough of their stories. They become very knowledgeable about their preferred authors and the kind of stories they like. They have even taken to hiding their favorite books, putting them on reserve as it were, to share with their home and school reading buddies. There is always a stack of books that have been recommended by the children waiting to be read.

### Daily Writing Opportunities

Daily opportunities to write are also a crucial part of the language program. As they encode their words in print, children learn about the shapes and sounds of letters and words. They turn to the books they have read to find out how to spell words they need. Books are the source of much of the children's knowledge about print. Yet a literature-rich classroom offers the child more than just concepts about print. Literature provides the stepping stone for their progress as writers. There are writerly ways of telling stories that differ from every day oral language, and it is the children's experiences of literature that introduce them to this more formal language. As Patrick said in his story about a dinosaur family, "The children played. The day passed on." As Margaret Meek says, it is the texts that teach.

Books offer children ideas for their own personal writing, models to copy as they seek to put their ideas on paper, and answers to the many questions they need to address as they write on nonfiction topics. We feel it is critical that children be given abundant opportunities to write in some fashion everyday. For children, as for adults, writing is a process during which they attempt to produce a document that reflects their thinking, their feelings, and their knowledge. The children's knowledge of books and their various styles helps these budding authors find a voice that suits the ideas they wish to convey to an audience.

Creating pattern books is favored by young children. Initially we read a number of pattern books to the group and listened as individual children shared such books with us. We examined the characteristics of the patterns such as their repeating or rhyming elements. We suggested that the children make their own pattern books using the same format, but selecting a topic of interest to them. Thus, George at Halloween wrote,

"Ghost, Ghost What Do You See?
I see a monster looking at me.
Monster, monster what do you see?
I see a vampire looking at me."

After hearing a series of fairy tales read to the class, a group of five girls decided to retell their favorite of the lot. *Hansel and Gretel* was their choice. Considerable time was spent by this group deciding the order of the retelling and who would produce which picture and accompanying text. The children took special care to vary their illustrative style to suit the text of each part of the story so the happy parts were done in bright bold colors and the sad parts were done in dark, gloomy colors.

### Encouraging Reluctant Writers

Why does a particular child not want to write? Is it because the child has difficulty forming the letters? If so, we would suggest the use of the computer. If this is not possible, consider sharing the task of writing with the child. Have the child begin the composition and when you see he or she is tiring take over the task yourself. Continue in this manner until the story is completed.

Another technique is to pair reluctant writers with children who have no difficulty putting pencil to paper. The composition is a shared endeavor. A buddy writing system, whereby an older child scribes for a younger writer, is also an effective strategy to use with children whose fine motor skills are slow to develop.

For the child who says, "I don't know what to write about!" there are other strategies that may be employed. Have the children make a list of all the areas in which they think they are an expert. Everyone thinks they are an expert about something! From this list the children are able to select a topic that they can begin to research. Team them with a writing partner who will listen to initial ideas, offer practical suggestions, act as a critical but supportive audience for first drafts, and help edit final drafts for publishing.

### Keeping Track of Progress in Writing

To keep track of the children's progress in writing we use writing folders, two for each child. One is for current work and is kept in a hanging file folder near the writing table. Each piece of work is dated and any conference notes or changes in the children's print literacy that we observe are noted on the back of the work. When a piece of writing is finished we store it in another file folder that is kept in a filing cabinet. These finished pieces of work form the basis for our reporting to parents and for the program evaluations that we make regularly for each child. A TIP — BUY A DATE STAMP AND KEEP THE WORK IN DATED SEQUENTIAL ORDER SO THAT IT IS EASIER TO SEE ANY PATTERNS THAT MIGHT BE DEVELOPING. Any writing that goes home does so in the form of a book, properly edited and published. This alleviates the problem of parents' seeing unedited work and inappropriately compelling the child to correct it.

## Conclusion

Reading and writing are the heart and soul of the primary classroom. Good practice is a delicate act of balance. We combine teaching methods which offer children choices within a framework of teacher decision-making; meaningful encounters with text are balanced with direct instruction that makes text accessible; activities which empower children to find their voices also offer adults a place to guide and instruct. When we let literature into a classroom we also let in ideas: painful, provoking, emotional, and stimulating. We allow children opportunitiies to develop their opinions and to become decision makers. We give them the power of literacy as a tool for their thinking. Real books — better books — are not an option, they are a necessity.

# A BIBLIOGRAPHY OF "BETTER" BOOKS

This bibliography of children's books is intended as a guideline for teachers who wish to sort their classroom collections into levels. Beginning with the easiest books, we have organized our selection into categories that offer children choice and a breadth of reading experience at each level as they practise and develop fluency. These are books that we have found and used. Where U.S. publishers differ from Canadian, the publisher in parenthesis is the U.S. one. Some of the books are older titles, and may only be available through libraries. Books are continuously going out of print, and it is difficult to keep a booklist absolutely current. The important thing is to begin with the books that you have available, sort them into categories, and build from there.

## Concept Books: Level One

Ahlberg, Janet and Allan. *Yum Yum.* Viking Kestrel, 1984.

Burningham, John. *First Words.* Walker Books, 1984.

_____ *Wobble Pop.- Cluck Baa.- Sniff Shout.- Slam Bang.- Jangle Twang.-Numbers Book* .Walker Books, 1988.

Boyle, Alison. *Counting Suprises. - Alphabet Suprises.* MacDonald, 1987.

Butler, Andrea. *Whose List Is This?* Goodyear Books, 1996.

Crews, Donald. *Truck.* Penguin, 1985.

_____ *Harbor.* Morrow, 1987.

_____ *Flying.* Greenwillow, 1989.

_____ (other titles available).

Ehlert, Lois. *Color Zoo.* Lippincott, 1989. (Harper Row, 1989.)

Ehlert, Lois. *Fish Eyes: A Book You Can Count On.* Harcourt Brace,1990.

_____ *Eating the Alphabet.* Voyager Books, 1989.

Emberley, Rebecca. *Jungle Sounds. - City Sounds.* Little Brown, 1989.

Fleming, Denise. *Count! Henry Holt,* 1992.

Hammond, Franklin. *Ten Little Ducks. Groundwood/Douglas and McIntyre, 1992.*

Harris,Pamela. *Looking at Opposites.* - Hot Cold Shy Bold. Kids Can Press, 1995.

Hoban, Tana. *I Read Signs.* Mulberry, 1983. (Morrow, 1987.)

_____ *What Is It?*

_____ *One, Two, Three.* Greenwillow, 1985.

_____ *Panda, Panda.* Greenwillow, 1986.

_____ *Over Under and Through.* Macmillan 1986.

_____ *Is It Red? Is It Yellow? Is It Blue?* Mulberry Books, 1987.

_____ *Count and See.* Macmillan, 1972.

Hutchins, Pat. *One Hunter.* Penguin, 1980. (Greenwillow, 1982.)

Inkpen, Mick. *Kipper's Book of Colors.* Hodder Children's Books, 1994.

_____ *Opposites.* 1994.- *Weather.* 1994.-*Counting.* 1994.

Maris, Ron. *My Book* . Penguin, 1986.

McMillan, Bruce. *One, Two, One Pair! Scholastic, 1991.*

Miller, Margaret. *Whose Hat?* Mulberry Books, 1997.

Ormerod, Jan. *Reading. - Sleeping. -* Walker Books, 1985.

Oxenbury, Helen. *I Touch.- I Hear.- I See. - I Can.* Walker Books, 1985. (Random, 1985.)

_____ *Numbers of Things. ABC of Things.* Collins Picture Lions, 1987.

Pienkowsi, Jan. *Colors.- Shapes.- ABC.* Penguin, 1983. (Simon and Schuster, 1989.)

_____ *Homes. - Weather. - Sizes.- Time.* Penguin, 1983. (Messner, 1983.)

_____ *Numbers. - Faces.* Penguin, 1983.

_____ *Zoo. - Farm.* Penguin, 1983. (David and Charles, 1985.)

Rathmann, Peggy. *Goodnight Gorilla.* Putnam, 1996.

Wood, A.J. *Animal Opposites. Templar, 1987.*

Walker, Steven. *Heads and Tails.* Puffin Books, 1996.

Ziefert, Harriet. *Cock-a-Doodle-Doo! - All Clean! - All Gone! - Run! Run!* Harper and Row, 1986.


## Concept Books: Level Two

Ahlberg, Janet and Allan. *The Baby's Catalogue.* Penguin, 1984. (Little Brown, 1986.)

Alexander, Martha. *You're Adorable.* Candlewick Press, 1994.

Boyton, Sandra. *Hippos Go Berserk.* Aladdin Paperbacks, 1996.

Butterfield, Moira. *Peekaboo Baby!* Zigzag Publishing Ltd. 1995.

Falwell, Cathryn. *Feast For 10.* Clarion Books, 1993.

Greenfield, Eloise. *Aaron and Gayla's Counting Book* Black Butterfly Children's Books, 1993.

Hansard, Peter. *Wag Wag Wag.* Candlewick Press, 1993.

Hayes, Sarah. *Nine Ducks Nine.* Walker Books, 1990.

Hutchins, Pat. *One Hunter.* Penguin, 1980. (Greenwillow, 1982.)

Kusagak, Michael. *Arvaarluk*. Annick Press, 1996.

_____ *My Arctic 1,2,3*. Annick Press, 1996.

Linden, Anne Marie. *One Smiling Grandma*. Picture Mammoth, 1996.

Sardegna, Jill. *K is for Kiss Goodnight*. Bantam Doubleday, Dell Books for Young Readers, 1996.


## Alphabet Books

Anno, M. *Anno's Alphabet*. Thomas Crowell, 1974.

Bannatyne-Cugnet, Jo. *A Prairie Alphabet*. Tundra Books. 1992.

Dodson, Peter. *An Alphabet of Dinosaurs*. Byron Preiss Visual, 1995.

Feelings, Muriel. *Swahili Alphabet Book*. Puffin Pied Piper, 1981.

Hague, Michael. *Alphabears: An ABC Book*. Holt Rinehart and Winston,1984.

Harrison, Ted. *A Northern Alphabet*. Tundra Books, 1982.

Isadora, Rachel. *City Scene from A to Z* .Mulberry Books, 1983.

Jordan, Martin and Tanis. *Amazon Alphabet*. Kingfisher, 1997.

Lessac, F. *Caribbean Alphabet*. Macmillan Caribbean, 1989.

Martin, Jr., Bill. *Chicka Chicka Boom Boom ABC*. Simon &Schuster, 1989.

Musgrove, M. *Ashanti to Zulu: African Traditions*. Dial, 1976.

Owens, M. B. *A Caribou Alphabet*. Firefly Books, 1988.

Rankin, L. *The Handmade Aphabet* Dial, 1991.

Shannon, George. *Tomorrow's Alphabet*. Greenwillow Books, 1996.

Thornhill, Jan. *The Wildlife ABC. - A Nature Alphabet*. Greey de Pencier Books, 1994.

Van Allsburg, Chris. *The Z was Zapped*. Houghton Mifflin, 1987.


## Wordless Picture Books

Aruego, Jose. *Look What I Can Do*. Scribner, 1971. (Macmillan, 1988.)

Banyai, Istvan. *REM (Rapid Eye Movement)* Viking, 1997.

Briggs, Raymond. *The Snowman*. Hamilton, 1978. (Faber & Faber, 1987.) Random, 1978.)

Goodall, John. *Adventures of Paddy Pork*. Harcourt Brace Jovanovich, 1968.

_____ *The Story of a Castle*. Andre Deutsch, 1987. (Macmillan, 1986.)

Hughes, Shirley. *Up and Up*. Penguin, 1981. (Lothrop, 1986.)

Hoban, Tana. *Is it Larger? Is it Smaller?* Mulberry Books, 1997.

*Shapes, Shapes, Shapes.* Mulberry Books, 1996.

Mayer, Mercer. *A Boy, A Dog and a Frog and a Friend.* Doubleday, 1978.

McCully, Emily Arnold. *School.* Harper Row, 1987.

_____ *Picnic.* Harper & Row, 1989.

Ormerod, Jan. *Sunshine.* Kestrel Books, 1981. (Penguin, 1984.)

_____ *Moonlight.* Kestrel Books, 1982. (Penguin, 1984.)

Prater, John. *The Gift.* Viking Kestrel, 1986. (Penguin, 1987.)

Sasaki, Isao. *Snow.* Viking, 1982.

Spier, Peter. *Peter Spier's Rain.* Doubleday, 1987.

Turkle, Brinton. *Deep In the Forest.* Dutton, 1976.

Widsmith, Brian. *Applebird.* Oxford, 1987.


## Pattern Books Level One

Asch, Frank. *I Can Blink. - I Can Roar.* Kids Can Press, 1985. (Crown, 1986.)

Barton, Byron. *Where's the Bear?* Penguin, 1984.

Buttonwood, Betsy. *Rockets.* Let Me Read: Good Year Books,1996.

Campbell, Rod. *Dear Zoo.* Penguin 1987. (Macmillan, 1986.)

_____*Oh Dear! Piper Books, 1989. (Macmillan, 1986.)*

Druce, Arden. *Witch, Witch Come to My Party.* Child's Play, 1991.

Duffy, Dee Dee. *Barnyard Tracks.* Boyds Mills Press, 1992.

_____*Forest Tracks.* Boyds Mills Press, 1996.

Gomi, Taro. *Shadows.* Heian International, 1981.

Hawkins, Colin. *What's the Time Mr. Wolf?* Collins Picture Lions, 1985.

Hill, Eric. *Where's Spot?* Putnam, 1980. (Interlink, 1988.)

Lewis Patrick, Denise. *I Can Count.* Golden Books, 1996.

Maris, Ron. *Better Move On Frog.* Collins, 1984.

Martin, Jr., Bill and Carle, Eric. *Brown Bear, Brown Bear What Do You See?* Holt Rhinehart 1983. (Henry Holt, 1983.)

_____ *Polar Bear, Polar Bear, What Do You Hear?* Holt & Co., 1991.

Murphy, Mary. *I Like it When....* Harcourt Brace, 1997.

Peek, Merle. *Mary Wore Her Red Dress and Henry Wore His Green Sneakers.* Clarion Books, 1985.

Quinlan, Patricia. *Baby's Feet.* Annick Press, 1996.

Rees, Mary. *Ten In A Bed.* Little Mammoth, 1989.

Roffey, Maureen. *Home Sweet Home.* Pan, 1985. (Putnam, 1983.)

Stobbs, William. *Gregory's Dog.* Oxford University Press, 1987.

Tafuri, Nancy. *Have You Seen My Duckling?* Penguin, 1986. (Greenwillow, 1984.)

Wildsmith, Brian. *Cat on the Mat. - All Fall Down. - Toot Toot.* Oxford University Press, 1987.

Wood, Leslie. *My Dog Called Mischief. - Bump, Bump, Bump.* Oxford University Press, 1987.

Williams, Sue. *I Went Walking.* Voyager Books, 1989.

Ziefert, Harriet and Smith, Mavis. *Going on a Lion Hunt.* Penguin, 1989.


## Pattern Books Level Two

Armstrong, Jennifer. *The Snowball.* Random House, 1996.

Artell, Mike. *Big Long Animal Song.* Good Year Books, 1996.

Burton, Katherine. *One Grey Mouse.* Kids Can Press, 1995.

Butler, Andrea. *Recycling Dump.* Let Me Read: Good Year Books, Scott Foresman, 1994.

Carle, Eric. *The Very Busy Spider.* Philomel, 1984.

Charles, N.N. *What Am I? Looking Through Shapes at Apples and Grapes.* Blue Sky Press , 1994.

Fleming, Denise. *In the Small, Small Pond.* Henry Holt & Co., 1993.

_____ *Barnyard Banter.* Scholastic, 1994.

_____*Where Once There was a Wood.* Henry Holt & Co., 1996.

Fox, Mem and Goodman, Vivienne. *Guess What?* Voyager Books, Harcourt Brace & Co. 1995. (Omnibus Books, 1988.)

Hawkins, Colin & Jacqui. *I Know An Old Lady Who Swallowed a Fly.* Little Mammoth, 1989.

Jonas, Ann. *Now We Can Go.* Greenwillow, 1986.

Jorgensen, Gail and Mullins, Patricia. *Crocodile Beat.* Scholastic Inc., 1995. (Macmillan, 1988.)

Kalan, Robert. *Rain.* Mulberry Books, 1991.,

Nichol, b.p. *Once: A Lullaby.* Black Moss Press, 1983. (Greenwillow, 1986.)

Tafuri, Nancy. *Spots, Feathers, and Curly Tails.* Greenwillow, 1988.

_____ *The Ball Bounced.* Morrow, 1989.

Wildsmith, Brian. - *What a Tale. - My Dream.* Oxford University Press, 1987.

## First Steps

Ahlberg, Allan and Mcnaughton, Colin. *Red Nose Readers* (Red Series) : *Help! - Jumping. - Make a Face. - Big Bad Pig. - Fee Fi Fo Fum.- Bear's Birthday. - So Can I. Random House, 1985.*

Barton, Byron. *Building a House.* Penguin, 1984. (Greenwillow, 1981.)

_____ *Airport.* Penguin, 1986. (Harper Row, 1987.)

_____ *Trucks.* Penguin, 1986. (Harper & Row, 1986.)

_____ *I Want to be an Astronaut.* Scholastic Inc., 1989. (Harper & Row, 1988.)

_____ *Dinosaurs Dinosaurs.* Harper Collins, 1989.

_____ *Where's Al.* Clarion Books, 1972. (Houghton Mifflin, 1989.)

Berenstain, Stan and Jan. *Inside Outside Upside Down.* Random House, 1968.

Brenner, Colin. *Good News.* Bantam Little Rooster Book, 1991.

Browne, Anthony. *I Like Books.* Walker Books, 1988. (Knopf, 1989.)

_____ *Things I Like.* Walker Books, 1989. (Knopf, 1988.)

Bruna, Dick. *I Can Read.* Methuen, 1969.

Burningham, John. *The School. - The Baby.- The Blanket.* Jonathan Cape 1983, (Harper Row, 1976.)

Campbell, Rod. *Henry's Busy Day.* Viking Kestrel, 1984.

Christelow, Eileen. *Five Little Monkeys Jumping on the Bed.* Clarion Books, 1989.

Cobb, Annie. *B is for Books.* Random House, 1996.

Connor, Coker Deborah. *I Like Me.* Golden Books, 1995.

Dodds, Siobhan. *Elizabeth Hen. - Charles Tiger.* Collins Picture Lions, 1989. (Little Brown, 1988.)

Dr. Seuss. *Foot Book.* Random House, 1968.

Drawson, Blair. *I Like Hats.* Scholastic Inc. 1980.

Eastman, P.D. *Go Dog Go.* Random House, 1961.

Galdone, Paul. *Three Little Kittens.* Clarion Books, 1986.

Garland, Sarah. *Doing the Washing.* Penguin, 1984.

_____ *Going Shopping. - Having a Picnic.* Penguin, 1986.

_____ *Coming to Tea.* Penguin, 1987.

Gomi, Taro. *Spring is Here.* Fitzhenry & Whiteside, 1989. (Chronicle Books, 1989.).

Grindley, Sally. *Four Black Puppies.* Walker Books, 1987

Guthrie, Woody. *Mail Myself to You.* Good Year Books, 1994.

Hunia, Fran. *Oops.* Ashton-Scholastic, 1984.

Jonas, Ann. *Where Can it Be? Greenwillow, 1986.*

Inkpen, Mick. *If I Had a Pig*. Macmillan, 1988. (Little Brown, 1988.)

Isadora, Rachel. *I Touch*. Collins Picture Lions, 1987. (Greenwillow, 1985.)

Lewis Patrick, Denise. *See What I Can Do*. Golden Books, 1996.

Lewison, Wendy. *Mud*. Random House, 1990.

Lindgren, Barbro & Erikssen, Eva. *Sam's Car. - Sam's Biscuit. - Sam's Teddy*. Methuen, 1984.

Maris, Ron. *Are You There Bear?* Penguin, 1986. (Greenwillow, 1985.)

Mark, Jan. *Fur*. Walker Books, 1986.

McKee, David. *Not Now Bernard*. Beaver Books, 1987. ( Penguin, 1986.)

Moss, Sally and Meredith Thomas. *Peter's Painting*. Mondo , 1995.

Mueller, Virginia. *Monster Can't Sleep*. Whitman, 1986.

O'Connor, Jane. *The Teeny, Tiny Woman*. Random House, 1986.

Ormerod, Jan. *Dad's Back. - Messy Baby*. Walker Books, 1985. (Lothrop, 1985.)

Rockwell, Anne. *On Our Vacation*. Puffin Unicorn, 1994.

Roffey, Maureen. *Look There's My Hat!* Pan, 1986. (Putnam, 1985.)

Robinson, Faye. *Meet My Mouse*. Good Year Books, 1996.

Satin Capucilli, Alyssa. *Biscuit*. Harper Trophy, 1996.

Shaw, Charles. *It Looked Like Spilt Milk*. Harper & Row, 1988.

Strickland, Paul and Henrietta. *Dinosaur Roar*. Doubleday, 1996.

Taylor, Judy and Cartwright, Reg. *My Dog. - My Cat*. Walker Books, 1987. (Macmillan, 1989.)

Titherington, Jeanne. *Pumpkin Pumpkin*. Greenwillow, 1986.

Vaughan, Marcia. *The Secret Friend*. Good Year Books, 1996.

Watanabe, Shigeo. *How Do I Eat It?* Penguin, 1982.

_____ *Hello How Are You?* Penguin, 1984.

_____ *I'm Going For a Walk*. Penguin, 1986.

West, Colin. *Buzz, Buzz, Buzz Went Bumblebee*. Candlewick Press, 1996.

Wildsmith, Brian. *The Island. - If I Were You*. Oxford University Press, 1987.

Wolff, Ashley. *Only The Cat Saw*. Penguin, 1988. (Putnam, 1985.)

Wood, Leslie. *The Frog and the Fly. - Tom and his Tractor*. Oxford University Press, 1987.

Ziefert, Harriet. *When the TV Broke*. Puffin, 1993.

_____ *A New House for Mole and Mouse*. Puffin, 1987.

## Step A Little Further

Ahlberg, Allan and Macnaughton, Colin. *Red Nose Readers.* (Yellow Series): *Crash Bang Wallop! - Me and My Friends. - Push the Dog. - Shirley's Shop's.* Random House, 1985.

Arnold, Marsha. *Quick, Quack, Quick!* Random House, 1996.

Asch, Frank. *Just Like Daddy.* Prentice Hall, 1981.

_____ *The Last Puppy.* Prentice Hall, 1983.

Bang, Molly. *Ten, Nine, Eight.* Penguin, 1985. (Greenwillow, 1983.)

Bonsall, Crosby. *Mine's The Best.* Harper Row, 1984.

Breinburg, Petronella. *My Brother Sean.* Penguin, 1986.

Brandenburg, Franz. *I Wish I Was Sick Too.* Greenwillow, 1976.

Brown, Ruth. *A Dark Dark Tale.* Hippo Books/ Scholastic, 1985. (Dial Books for Young Readers, 1984.)

Bruna, Dick. *I Can Read More.* Methuen, 1969 (Price Stern, 1984.)

Burningham, John. *The Rabbit. - The Cupboard. - The Friend.* Jonathan Cape, 1983. (Harper Row, 1976.)

Butler, Elizabeth. *Surprise.* Good Year Book, 1996.

Carlson, Nancy. *I Like Me.* Puffin, 1990

Coxen, Michele. *Where's My Kitten?* Puffin Books, 1996.

Donnelly, Lisa. *Dinosaur Day.* Scholastic Inc., 1987.

Ehlert, Lois. *Growing Vegetable Soup.* Harcourt Brace, 1987.

_____ *Planting a Rainbow.* Harcourt Brace, 1988.

_____ *Feathers For Lunch.* Harcourt Brace, 1990.

Ginsburg, Mirra. *Three Kittens.* Crown, 1973.

_____ *Where Does the Sun Go at Night?* Mulberry, 1981. (Greenwillow, 1980.)

_____ *The Chick and the Duckling.* Macmillan, 1988.

Ginsburg, Mirra and Tafuri, Nancy. *Across The Stream.* Penguin, 1985. (Greenwillow, 1982.)

Gomi, Taro. *Coco Can't Wait.* Penguin, 1985.

Harper, Anita and Hellard, Susan. *It's Not Fair.* Penguin, 1986. (Putnam,1986.)

_____ *Just a Minute!* Penguin 1987. (Putnam,1987.)

Hayes, Sarah. *This is the Bear.* Walker Books, 1986. (Harper & Row, 1986.)

Hill, Eric. *Spot's First Walk.* Puffin,

Hinds, Mignon, P. *My Best Friend.* Golden Books, 1996.

*What I Want To Be.* Golden Books, 1996.

Hutchins, Pat. *Rosie's Walk*. Collins, 1968. (Macmillan, 1971.)

Hughes, Shirley. *Bouncing. - Chatting. - Giving. - Hiding.* Candlewick Press,1995.

Jewell, Nancy. *Two Silly Trolls. - Silly Times with Two Silly Trolls.* Harper Trophy, 1996.

Jones, Maurice. *I'm Going on a Dragon Hunt.* Penguin, 1988. (Macmillan, 1987.)

Kraus, Robert. *Herman the Helper Lends a Hand.* Windmill, 1974.

Kraus, Robert and Aruego, Jose. *Whose Mouse Are You?* Collins, 1970. (Macmillan, 1972.)

_____ *Where Are You Going Little Mouse?* Mulberry, 1986. (Morrow, 1989.)

Krasny Brown, Laurie. *Rex and Lilly Family Time. - Rex and Lilly Playtime. Rex and Lilly Schooltime.* Little Brown & Co., 1995.

Loewen, Iris. *My Kokum Called Today.* Pemmican, 1993.

Lung, Earlene. *Gone Fishing.* Houghton Mifflin, 1984.

Maris, Ron. *I Wish I Could Fly.* Penguin, 1988. (Greenwillow, 1987.)

_____ Is Anyone Home? Greenwillow, 1985.

Morris, Ann and Ken Heyman *Bread Bread Bread.* Lothrop, Lee and Shepard, 1989.

Piers, Helen. *Hamster is Hiding. - Kittens in the Kitchen. - Puppy in the Park. - Goat in the Garden.* (and other titles). Methuen, 1984.

Rockwell, Anne. *Boats.* Dutton, 1985.

_____ *Toolbox.* Penguin, 1982. (Macmillan, 1971.)

Rockwell, Harlow. *My Nursery School.* Penguin, 1974.

_____ *My Kitchen.*Greenwillow, 1980.

Rose, Gerald. *Ah! Said Stork.* Picturemac, 1986.

Silverman, Martin. *My Tooth is Loose.* Puffin Books, 1994.

Walsh, Ellen Stoll. *Mouse Paint.* Voyager Books, 1989.

Watanabe, Shigeo. *How Do I Put it on ?* Putnam, 1984.

_____ *I'm the King of the Castle!* Putnam, 1982.

_____ *I Can Build a House!* Putnam, 1985.

_____ *I'm Playing with Papa!* Putnam, 1986.

West, Colin. *Pardon? Said the Giraffe.* Harper Row,

Wildsmith, Brian. *Giddy Up.* Oxford University Press, 1987.

Wise Brown, Margaret. *Goodnight Moon.* Harper Collins, 1947.

Ziefert, Harriet. Hello Reading! Series: *Nicky Upstairs and Down.*

_____ *Harry Takes a Bath.- Mike and Tony: Best Friends. - Thank you Nicky.* Penguin, 1987.

_____ *The Turnip.* Puffin Books, 1996.

_____ *The Princess and the Pea.* Puffin Books, 1996.

_____ *Let's Trade.* Puffin Books, 1996.

_____ *Follow Me.* Puffin Books, 1996.


## Step A Little Faster

Ahlberg, Janet and Allan. *Each Peach Pear Plum.* Collins, 1980. (Penguin, 1986.)

Allen, Pamela. *Who Sank the Boat?* Hamish Hamilton, 1982. (Putnam, 1985.)

Asch, Frank. *Bread and Honey.* Parents Magazine Press, 1981.

Brenner, Barbara. *The Plant That Kept On Growing.* Bantam Books,1996.

Brown, Ruth. *The Big Sneeze.* Collins, Beaver Books, 1986. (Lothrop, 1985.)

Burningham, John. *The Snow. - The Dog.* Jonathan Cape, 1983. (Harper & Row 1976.)

_____ *Would You Rather?* Collins, 1984. (Harper & Row, 1978.)

Chase, Edith Newlin & Reid, Barbara. *The New Baby Calf.* Scholastic, 1986.

Carle, Eric. *The Very Hungry Caterpillar.* Putnam, 1986.

Chorao, K. *Kate's Car. - Kate's Box. - Kate's Snowman. - Kate's Quilt.* Dutton, 1982.

Cocca-Leffler, Maryann. *What a Pest!* Grosset & Dunlap, 1994.

Dickinson, Mary. *Shan Helps Rani.* Andre Deutsch, 1990.

Eastman, P.D. *Are You My Mother?* Collins, 1962 (Random, 1967.)

Ehlert, Lois. *Nuts To You!* Harcourt Brace, 1993.

Fox, Mem. *Hattie and the Fox.* BradburyPress, 1987.

Garland, Sarah. *Tex the Cowboy.* Red Fox, 1997.

Ginsburg, Mirra and Barton, Byron. *Good Morning Chick.* Scholastic Inc., 1980. (Greenwillow,1980.)

Goodspeed, Peter. *A Rhinoceros Wakes Me Up in the Morning.* Penguin, 1984.

Gray, Nigel and Craig, Helen. *The One and Only Robin Hood.* Walker Books, 1987. (Little Brown, 1987.)

Hayes, Sarah. *The Bear and the Picnic.* Walker Books, 1986.

Hutchins, Pat. *Good-Night Owl.* Macmillan, 1972.

_____ *Happy Birthday Sam.* Penguin, 1981.

_____ *Titch.* Penguin, 1984.

_____ *You'll Soon Grow into Them, Titch* . Penguin, 1985.

_____ *Shrinking Mouse.* Greenwillow, 1997.

Jonas, Ann. *The Quilt.* Greenwillow, 1984.

_____ *The Trek.* Greenwillow, 1985.

_____ *When You Were a Baby.* Morrow,

_____ *Splash!* Mulberry Books, 1997.

Joyce, William. *George Shrinks.* Harper & Row, 1987.

Kraus, Robert. *Herman the Helper.* Windmill Books, 1974. (Simon & Schuster, 1987. Prentice Hall, 1987.)

Kraus, Robert and Aruego, Jose. *Leo The Late Bloomer.* Windmill Books, 1971. (Harper & Row, 1987.)

Kraus, Robert. *Come Out and Play Little Mouse.* Greenwillow, 1987.

Krauss, Ruth. *The Carrot Seed.* Harper & Row, 1945.

_____ *Is This You?* Scholastic, 1955.

Levinson, Riki and Goode, Diane. *I Go With My Family To Grandma's.* Dutton, 1986.

Lindbergh, Reeve. *What is the Sun?* Candlewick Press, 1996.

Lottridge, Celia. *One Watermelon Seed.* Oxford University Press, 1987.

Mayer, Mercer. *There's a Nightmare in My Closet.* Dial Books for Young Readers, 1976.

_____ *Just For You.* Golden Books, 1975.

_____ *Just Me and My Babysitter.* Golden Books, 1986.

_____ *Just Me and My Puppy.* Golden Books, 1985.

_____ *Just a Mess.* Golden Books, 1987.

McPhail, David. *Fix- It.* Unicorn, 1987. (Dutton, 1984.)

Morris, Ann and Heyman, Ken. *The Daddy Book.* Silver Press, 1996.

Natanani, Chiyoko. *Feeding Babies.* Penguin, 1983.

Nicoll, Helen and Pienkowski, Jan. *Meg and Mog.* Penguin, 1976.

_____ *Meg's Eggs. - Meg's Castle.* Penguin, 1975.

_____ *Mog's Mumps.* Penguin, 1979. (David & Charles, 1983.)

_____ *Mog at the Zoo.* Penguin, 1985.

_____ *Owl at School.* Penguin, 1986. (David & Charles, 1984.) (other titles avilable.)

Polushkin, Maria. *Mother, Mother I Want Another.* Crown, 1986.

Pomerantz, Charlotte; Aruego, Jose and Dewey, Ariane. *One Duck, Another Duck.* Penguin, 1984. (Greenwillow, 1984.)

Raffi. *Like Me and You.* Crown Publishers, 1994.

Rice, Eve, *Sam Who Never Forgets.* Penguin, 1980. (Greenwillow, 1977. Morrow, 1977.)

Riddell, Chris. *Ben and the Bear*. Walker Books, 1986. (Harper & Row, 1986.)

Rosen, Michael *We're Going on a Bear Hunt*. Walker Books, 1989.

Shaw, Nancy and Apple, Margot. *Sheep in a Jeep*. Houghton Mifflin, 1988.

\_\_\_\_\_ *Sheep on a Ship*. Houghton Mifflin, 1989.

\_\_\_\_\_ *Sheep in a Shop*. Houghton Mifflin, 1991.

\_\_\_\_\_ *Sheep Out to Eat. - Sheep Take a Hike*. Houghton Mifflin, 1992.

Stadler, John. *Hooray For Snail*! Harper & Row, 1985.

\_\_\_\_\_ *Snail Saves the Day*. Harper Collins, 1985.

Stinson, Kathy. *Red Is Best*. Annick Press, 1982. (Firefly Books, 1982.)

\_\_\_\_\_ *Big or Little*. Annick Press, 1983. (Firefly Books,1983.)

Sutton, Eve. *My Cat Likes to Hide in Boxes*. Penguin, 1978.

Ward, Heather Patricia. *I Promise I'll Find You*. Firefly Books, 1997.

Wells, Rosemary. *Noisy Nora*. Dial Books for Young Readers, 1980.

Wood, Don and Audrey. *The Napping House*. Harcourt, 1984.

Wildsmith, Brian. *What the Moon Saw*. Oxford University Press, 1978.

Wise Brown, Margaret. *Goodnight Moon*.

## Taking Off

Ahlberg, Janet and Allan. *Peepo!* Penguin, 1983.

Asch, Frank. *Sand Cake*. Parents Magazine, 1987. (Crown, 1987.)

\_\_\_\_\_ *Bear Shadow*. Parents Magazine Press, 1985.

\_\_\_\_\_ *Bear's Bargain*. Parents Magazine Press, 1985.

Blake, Quentin. *Mister Magnolia*. Collins, 1987.

\_\_\_\_\_ *All Join In*. Red Fox, 1992.

Bonsall, Crosby. *Who's Afraid of the Dark?* Harper & Row, 1985.

Brandenburg, Franz. *I Don't Feel Well*. Penguin, 1982.

Brenner, Barbara. *The Color Wizard*. Bantam Books, 1990.

Browne, Anthony. *Through the Magic Mirror*. Picturemac, 1987.

Burningham, John. *Mr. Gumpy's Outing*. Penguin, 1984.(Henry Holt, 1971.)

\_\_\_\_\_ *Mr. Gumpy's Motor Car*. Penguin, 1983. (Harper & Row, 1976.)

\_\_\_\_\_ *Come Away From The Water Shirley*. Collins, 1983. (Harper & Row, 1983.)

Carle, Eric. *The Secret Birthday Message*. Harper & Row, 1986.

Degen, Bruce. *Jamberry*. Harper & Row, 1985.

DeMorest, Chris L . *Benedict Finds a Home*. Methuen, Pocket Bears,1984.

De Paola, Tomie. *The Knight and the Dragon*. Putnam, 1980.

Falconer, Elizabeth. *Three Little Witches*. Collins Picture Lions, 1989.

Hearn, Emily, and Collins, Heather. *Whoosh! I Heard a Sound*. Annick Press,1983.

Hoff, Syd. *Danny and the Dinosaur*. Harper & Row, 1978.

_____ *The Horse in Harry's Room*. Harper & Row, 1985.

Holtzman, Caren. *No Fair!* Scholastic Inc., 1997.

Hurd, Edith Thacher. *Johnny Lion's Book*. Harper & Row, 1985.

Hutchins, Pat. *Tom and Pat*. Penguin, 1972.

_____ *Don't Forget the Bacon*. Penguin, 1982.

_____ *Clocks and More Clocks*. MacMillan, 1970.

_____ *The Doorbell Rang*. Greenwillow, 1986.

Jonas, Ann. *The Round Trip*. Greenwillow, 1983.

Kasza, Keiko. *The Wolf's Chicken Stew*. G.P.Putnam's, 1987.

Keats, Ezra Jack. *Over in the Meadow*. Scholastic, Inc. 1971.

Lobel, Arnold. *Mouse Tales*. Harper & Row, 1978.

_____ *Frog and Toad are Friends*. Harper & Row, 1979.

_____ *Owl at Home*. Harper & Row, 1982.

_____ *Days with Frog and Toad*. Harper & Row, 1984.

Mahy, Margaret. *Seventeen Kings and Forty-Two Elephants*. Collins Picture Lions, 1979. (Dial Books for Young Readers, 1987.)

Minarik, Else. *A Kiss for Little Bear*. (and other titles). Harper & Row, 1968.

Murray, Jill. *Peace at Last*. Dial Books for Young Readers, 1980.

O'Connor, Jane. *Nina, Nina, Ballerina*. Grosset & Dunlap, 1993.

Oram, Hiawyn and Kitimara, Satoshi. *Angry Arthur*. Penguin, 1984. (Dutton, 1989).

Pinkwater, Daniel. *I Was a Second Grade Werewolf*. Dutton, 1985.

Ross, Tony. *I'm Coming to Get You!* Dial Books, 1987.

Sadler, Marilyn. *The Parakeet Girl*. Random House, 1997.

Thaler, Mike. *There's a Hippopotamus Under My Bed*. Avon Books, 1978.

_____ *A Hippopotamus Ate the Teacher*. Avon Books, 1981.

_____*Upside Down*. Avon Books, 1986.

Waddell, Martin. *Farmer Duck*. Candlewick Press, 1996.


## You're Away

Ahlberg, Allan. *Happy Families*. (Series, 12 titles). Penguin/Kestrel Books, 1981.

_____ *Funnybones*. Collins, 1982. (Greenwillow, 1981.)

Bernier-Grand, Carmen. *Juan Bobo: Four Folk Tales from Puerto Rico. Harper Trophy, 1994.*

Bogart, Jo Ellen. *Daniel's Dog*. North Winds Press, 1990.

Bonsall, Crosby. *The Case of the Cat's Meow*. Harper & Row, 1978.

_____ *The Case of the Scaredy Cats*. Harper Trophy, 1984.

Brandenberg, Franz. *Nice New Neighbours*. Scholastic Inc., 1980. (Greenwillow, 1977.)

Brewster, Patience. *Too Many Puppies*. Scholastic Inc., 1997.

Briggs, Raymond. *Jim and the Beanstalk*. Penguin, 1973. (Putnam, 1989.)

Briggs, Raymond and Vipont, Elfrida. *The Elephant and the Bad Baby. Penguin, 1971.*

Browne, Anthony. *Gorilla. - A Walk in the Park*. Methuen, 1985. (Knopf, 1985.)

_____ *Willy the Wimp*. Methuen, 1986. (Knopf, 1985.)

_____ *Bear Goes to Town*. Doubleday,

Brown, Marc. *Arthur Goes To Camp*. Littlebrown & Co. 1982.

_____ *Arthur's Chicken Pox*. Little Brown and Co. 1994. (and other titles)

Brown, Ruth. *The Picnic*. Anderson Press, 1997.

Caines, Jeanette. *Just Us Women*. Harper & Row, 1982.

Carle, Eric. *The Grouchy Ladybug*. Harper & Row, 1986.

_____ *The Very Quiet Cricket*. Philomel Books, 1990.

Carlson, Nancy. *Harriet and the Garden*. (and other titles). Penguin, 1985.

Cohen, Miriam and Hoban, Lillian. *When Will I Read?* Dell, 1987.

Cole, Joanna. *Spiders Lunch: All About Garden Spiders*. 1995.

Debnan, Rosemary and Munoz, Claudio. *Runaway Fred*. Mammoth, 1997.

Fox, Mem. *Wilfred Gordon McDonald Partridge*. Penguin, 1987. (Kane-Miller Books, 1989.)

Freeman, Don. *Corduroy*. Penguin, 1976.

_____ *A Pocket for Corduroy*. Penguin, 1978.

Gerstein, Mordicai. *Arnold of the Ducks*. Harper & Row, 1985.

Giff, Patricia Reilly and Susanna Natti. *Today Was a Terrible Day. Penguin, 1980.*

Gilman, Phoebe. *Jillian Jigs*. Scholastic Inc. 1988.

Hautzig, Deborah. *Little Witch's Big Night*. Step-Into-Reading: Random House, 1987.

Hayes, Sarah and Ormerod, Jan. *Eat Up Gemma*. Walker Books, 1988. (Lothrop, 1988.)

Hoberman, Mary Ann and Fraser, Betty. *A House is a House for Me*. Penguin, 1982.

Hurd, Thacher. *Mama Don't Allow*. Harper & Row, 1985.

Isadora, Rachel. *Max*. Macmillan, 1976.

Keats, Ezra Jack. *The Snowy Day*. Penguin, 1976.

_____ *Whistle For Willie*. Penguin, 1976.

_____ *Peter's Chair*. Harper & Row, 1983.

Luttrell, Ida. *Milo's Toothache*. Puffin Books, 1997.

Mahy, Margaret. *The Boy Who Was Followed Home*. Dial Books for Young Readers, 1983.

McCully, Emily Arnold. *Two Grandmas — Double Trouble*. Harper Collins, 1988.

McMullan, Kate. *The Biggest Mouth in Baseball*. Grosset & Dunlap, 1993.

McNulty, Faith. *The Elephant Who Couldn't Forget*. Harper & Row, 1989.

McPhail, David. *Snow Lion*. Parents Magazine, 1987. (Crown, 1987.)

Milton, Joyce. *Gorillas: Gentle Giants of the Rainforest*. Random House, 1997.

Moore, Lillian.(retold by) *The Ugly Duckling*. Scholastic, 1987.

Munsch, Robert. *The Dark*. Annick Press, 1979. Firefly Books (Canada & the U.S.), 1984.

Nicklaus, Carol. *That's Not Chester*. Avon Books, 1975.

Novak, Matt. *Newt*. Harper Trophy, 1996.

Peppe, Rodney. *The Mice Who Lived in a Shoe*. Penguin, 1984. (Lothrop, 1982.)

Rice, Eve. *New Blue Shoes*. Penguin, 1979.

Rylant, Cynthia. *When I Was Young in the Mountains*. Dutton, 1985.

_____ *Henry and Mudge in Puddle Trouble*. (and other titles). Aladdin Paperback, 1987.

Sendak, Maurice. *Where The Wild Things Are*. Harper & Row, 1988.

Staunton, Ted and Kovalski, Maryann. *Puddleman*. Kids Can Press, 1983.

Stevens, Jane. *Old Bag of Bones: A Coyote Tale*. Holiday House, 1996.

Stinson, Kathy and McLoughlin, Mary. *Those Green Things*. Annick Press, 1985. (Firefly Books, 1985.)

Stren, Patti. *Hug Me*. Fitzhenry & Whiteside, 1977.

Thurman, Mark. *Two Pals on an Adventure*. (series)

_____ *Douglas the Elephant*.(series) NC Press, 1985.

Ungerer, Tomi. *The Three Robbers.* Atheneum Children's Books, 1962.(Macmillan, 1975)

Van Leeuwen, Jan. *Amanda Pig on Her Own.* (and other titles). Puffin,1991.

Wagner, Jenny. *John Brown, Rose and the Midnight Cat.* Penguin, 1980.

Wayne Von Konigslow, Andrea. *That's My Baby.* Annick Press, 1986.

Yolen, Jane. *Commander Toad in Space.* (and other titles). Coward McCann, 1984. (Putnam, 1980.)

Zion, Gene. *Harry the Dirty Dog.* Harper & Row, 1976.


## Getting Longer

Ahlberg, Janet and Allan. *Burglar Bill.* Collins, 1979.

_____ *The Jolly Postman.* Heinemann, 1986. (Little, Brown, 1986.)

Alexander, Sue. *World Famous Muriel. - World Famous Muriel and the Scary Dragon.* Dell, 1988.

Aliki. *We Are Best Friends.* Mulberry, 1982. (Greenwillow, 1982.)

Allard, Harry. *Miss Nelson is Missing.* Houghton Mifflin, 1985.

Arvaarluk Kusugak, Michael. *Baseball Bats for Christmas.* Annick Press, 1990.

Aubin, Michel, and Desputeaux, Helene. *The Secret Code.* James Lorimer & Co., 1987.

Avi. *Finding Providence.* Harper Trophy, 1997.

Blades, Ann. *Mary of Mile 18.* Tundra Books, 1971.

Blake, Quentin. *Patrick.* Penguin, 1970.

Blume, Judy. *The One in the Middle is the Green Kangaroo.* Dell, 1982. (Bradbury,1981.)

_____ *The Pain and the Great One.* Dell, 1985. (Bradbury, 1984.)

Bunting, Eve and Ronald Himmler. *Fly Away Home.* Clarion Books, 1991.

_____ *The Wall* .Clarion Books, 1990.

Bunting, Eve and Dias, David. *December.* Harcourt Brace, 1997.

Burningham, John. *Where's Julius?* Collins, 1988. (Crown, 1987.)

Byars, Betsy. *The Golly Sisters Go West. - Hooray for the Golly Sisters.* Harper Trophy, 1990.

_____ *The Golly Sisters Ride Again.* Harper Trophy, 1994.

Carrick, Carol and Donald. *Patrick's Dinosaurs.* Clarion Books, 1982. (Houghton Mifflin, 1983.)

_____ *What Happened to Patrick's Dinosaurs?* Clarion Books, 1984. (Ticknor & Fields, 1986.)

Carrier, Roch. *The Hockey Sweater*. Tundra Books, 1984.

Castor, Harriet. *Fat Puss and Friends*. Penguin, 1985.

Christian, Mary Blount. *Swamp Monsters*. Dial Books,1983.

Climo, Shirley and Heller, Ruth . *The Egyptian Cinderella*. Harper Collins, 1989.

Coerr, Eleanor. *The Josephina Story Quilt*. Harper Trophy, 1986.

_____ *Chang's Paper Pony*. Harper Trophy, 1990.

Cohen, Barbara. *The Carp in the Bathtub*. Kar-Ben Copies Inc., 1987.

Cohen, Miriam and Hoban, Lillian. *Liar, Liar, Pants on Fire!* Dell, 1987.(Greenwillow, 1985.)

_____ *See You Tomorrow, Charles*. Dell, 1989. (Greenwillow, 1983.)

Cooney, Barbara. *Miss Rumphius*. Viking Penguin, 1985.

_____ *Emily*. Viking, Penguin, 1992.

_____ *Eleanor*. Viking Penguin, 1996.

Cosby, Bill. Little Bill Books: *The Best Way to Play*.

_____ *The Meanest Thing to Say. The Treasure Hunt*. Scholastic Inc., 1997

Coville, Bruce and Katherine. *Sarah's Unicorn*. Harper & Row, 1985.

Cristaldi, Kathryn. *Princess Lulu Goes to Camp*. Grosset & Dunlap, 1997.

Deitz Shea, Pegi. *The Whispering Cloth: A Refugee's Story*. Boyds Mill Press, 1995.

Doppert, Kursa, and Monika. Trans. by Karen Englander. *The Streets are Free*. Annick Press, 1985.

Edwards, Dorothy. *My Naughty Little Sister Goes Fishing*. Penguin, 1985.

Eyvendson, Peter. *Red Parka Mary*. Pemmican, 1996.

Foreman, Michael. *Dinosaurs and All that Rubbish*. Penguin, 1974.

_____ *Long Neck and Thunderfoot*. Penguin, 1984.

_____ *War and Peas*. Penguin, 1987. (Harper & Row, 1974.)

Frazier, Deborah. *On the Day You were Born*. Harcourt Brace & Co., 1991.

Garret Bang, Molly. *Wiley and the Hairy Man*. Aladdin Paperbacks, 1987.

Godkin, Celia. *Wolf Island*. Fitzhenry and Whiteside, 1990. (W.H.Freeman, 1995.)

Greenburg, Dan. *The Zack Files*. (Series) Grosset & Dunlap, 1996.

_____ *Great-Grandpa's in the Litter Box.- Through the Medicine Cabinet. - A Ghost Named Wanda.- Zap! I'm a Mind Reader.- Dr. Jekyll, Orthodondist.*

_____ *Do They Give Frequent Flier Miles For Out of Body Travel?*

Greer, Gery and Ruddick, Bob. *Billy the Ghost and Me*. Harper Trophy, 1997.

Havill, Juanita. *Jamaica's Find*. Houghton Mifflin, 1986.

Hoffman, Mary and Binch, Caroline. *Amazing Grace*. Dial Books, 1991.
_____ *Grace and Family*. Dial Books, 1995.

Hughes, Shirley. *Dogger*. Collins Picture Lions, 1979. (Lothrop, 1988.)
_____ *Moving Molly*. Collins Picture Lions, 1981. (Prentice- Hall, 1982. Lothrop, 1988.)
_____ *Alfie Gets in First*. Collins Picture Lions, 1982. (Lothrop, 1982.)
_____ *Alfie's Feet*. Collins Picture Lions, 1984. (Morrow, 1988.)
_____ *Alfie Gives a Hand*. Collins Picture Lions, 1985. (Morrow, 1986.)

Johnson, Tony. *The First Day of School*. Scholastic, 1997.

Kellog, Stephen. *The Island of the Skog*. Dial Books,1976.

Kovalski, Maryann. *Brenda and Edward*. Kids Can Press, 1984.

Leaf, Munro. *The Story of Ferdinand*. Penguin, 1988.

Lewis, Thomas P. *Hill of Fire*. Harper & Row, 1983.

Marshall, Edward. *Fox and His Friends*. Dial Books, 1987.

Mayer, Marianna. *The Black Horse*. Dial Books, 1987.

McNaughton, Colin. *Captain Abdul's Pirate School*. Candlewick Press, 1994.

McNulty, Faith. *Listen to the Whales Sing*. Scholastic Inc., 1996.

Minarik, Else Holmelund. *No Fighting, No Biting*. Harper Trophy, 1986.

Monjo, F.N. *Drinking Gourd*. Harper & Row, 1983.

Muller, Robin. *Tatterhood*. Scholastic-TAB, 1984. North Winds Press, 1984.

Munsch, Robert. *The Paper Bag Princess*. Annick Press, 1980. Firefly Books (Canada and the U.S.), 1980.
_____ *Mud Puddle*. Annick Press, 1982. Firefly Books (Canada and the U.S.), 1982.
_____ *Love You Forever*. 1982. Firefly Books (Canada and the U.S.), 1982.
_____ *David's Father*. Annick Press, 1983. Firefly Books (Canada and the U.S.), 1983.
_____ *Millicent and the Wind*. Annick Press, 1984. Firefly Books (Canada and the U.S.), 1984.
_____ *Thomas' Snowsuit*. Annick Press, 1985. Firefly Books (Canada and the U.S.), 1985.

Munsch, Robert, and Kusugak, Michael. *A Promise is a Promise*. Annick Press, 1987. Firefly Books (Canada and the U.S.), 1988.

Nyul, Choi Sook. *The Best Older Sister*. Yearling, 1997.

O'Connor, Jane. *Molly the Brave and Me.* Random House, 1990.

Ormerod, Jan. *Eat Up, Gemma.* Walker Books, 1988.

Parish, Peggy. *Amelia Bedelia* (series). Scholastic Inc., 1970. (Harper & Row, 1983.)

\_\_\_\_\_ *Amelia Bedelia Goes Camping.* Avon Books, 1986.

\_\_\_\_\_ *Amelia Bedelia Helps Out.* Avon Books, 1997.

Peet, Bill. *The Ant and the Elephant.* Houghton Mifflin, 1980.

Pfister, Marcus. *The Rainbow Fish.* Pan Asian Publications,1995.

Potter, Beatrix. *The Tale of Peter Rabbit.* Frederick Warne, 1902.

Rathmann, Peggy. *Officer Buckle and Gloria.* ScholasticInc. 1995.

Rockwell, Anne and Harlow. *The Night We Slept Outside.* Macmillan, 1986.

Rey, H.A. *Curious George.* Houghton Mifflin. 1973.

Ringgold, Faith. *Aunt Harriet's Underground Railroad in the Sky.* Crown Publishers Inc. 1992.

Rose, Gerald. *The Tiger Skin Rug.* Penguin, 1981.

Ryan, John. *Pugwash and the Midnight Feast.- Pugwash and the Wreckers.* Penguin, 1986.

Rylant, Cynthia. *Mr. Putter and Tabby Series.* Harcourt Brace, 1997

\_\_\_\_\_ *Mr. Putter and Tabby Row the Boat.*

\_\_\_\_\_ *Mr. Putter and Tabby Fly the Plane.*

\_\_\_\_\_ *Mr. Putter and Tabby Walk the Dog.*

\_\_\_\_\_ *Mr. Putter and Tabby Pour the Tea.*

\_\_\_\_\_ *Mr. Putter and Tabby Bake the Cake.*

\_\_\_\_\_ *Mr. Putter and Tabby Pick the Pears.*

Sharmat, Marjorie Wienman. *Nate the Great* (and other titles). Dell, 1977. (Putman, 1972.)

Steig, William. *Sylvester and the Magic Pebble.* Windmill Books, 1969. (Simon and Schuster, 1988.)

\_\_\_\_\_ *Amos and Boris. - The Amazing Bone.* Penguin, 1977. (Farrar, Straus & Giroux, 1971, 1976.)

\_\_\_\_\_ *Dr. De Soto.* Scholastic Inc., 1982. ( A Sunburst Book, Farrar, Straus & Giroux, 1982.)

\_\_\_\_\_ *Gorky Rises.* A Sunburst Book, Farrar, Straus & Giroux, 1986.

Targ Brill, Marlene *Allen Jay and the Underground Railroad.* Carlorhoda Books Inc., 1997.

Turkle, Brinton. *Do Not Open.* Dutton, 1985.

Van Allsburg, Chris. *The Wreck of the Zephyr.* Houghton Mifflin, 1983.

Varley, Susan. *Badger's Parting Gifts.* Collins Picture Lions. 1985.

Wallace, Ian. *The Sandwich.* Kids Can Press, 1975.

Waterton, Betty. *A Salmon for Simon.* Douglas & McIntyre, 1987.

Wells, Rosemary. *Timothy Goes to School.* Dial Books., 1983.

Wildsmith Brian. *The Little Wood Duck.* Oxford University Press, 1987.

Yee, Paul. *Roses Sing on New Snow.* Groundwood, 1991.

_____ *The Ghost Train.* Groundwood, 1996.

Yeoman, John & Blake Quentin. *Mouse Trouble.* Penguin, 1976.

Young, Ed. *Lon Po Po : A Red Riding Hood Story From China. Philomel Books, 1989.*

Yuan-Liou Publishing Co., (no author), *Mouse Bride: A Chinese Folktale. 1994.*

Zolotow, Charlotte. *William's Doll. - My Grandson Lew.* Harper & Row, 1985.


## First Novels

Adler, David A. *The Fourth Floor Twins and the Skyscraper Parade.* Penguin, 1988.

_____ *Cam Jansen* (series) - *Cam Jansen and the Mystery of the UFO. - Cam Jansen and the Mystery of the Stolen Diamonds.* (and other titles.) Dell, 1982. (Puffin Books, 1997.)

Aiken, Joan. *Fog Hounds, Wind Cat, Sea Mice.* Piccolo, 1987.

Ardizzone, Edward and Aingelda. *The Little Girl and the Tiny Doll.* Young Puffin, 1979.

Avi. *Tom, Babette & Simon.* Avon Books, 1997.

Berends, Polly. *The Case of the Elevator Duck.* Random House, A Stepping Stone Book, 1989.

Blume, Judy. *Freckle Juice.* Dell, 1978.

_____ *Superfudge.* Dell, 1981.

_____ *Tales of a Fourth Grade Nothing.* Dell,

Brown, Jeff. *Flat Stanley.* Methuen, 1980. (Harper & Row, 1964.)

Buck, Pearl. *The Big Wave.* Harper & Row, 1986.

Bulla, Clyde Robert. *A Lion to Guard Us.* Scholastic Inc., 1983. (Harper & Row, 1989.)

_____ *The Chalk Box Kid.* Random House, A Stepping Stone Book,.1987.

_____ *White Bird.* Random House, A Stepping Stone Book,.1987.

Cameron, Ann. *Julian's Glorious Summer.* Random House, A Stepping Stone Book, 1987.

_____ *The Most Beautiful Place in the World*. Random House, 1988. (Knopf, 1988.)

_____ *Julian, Secret Agent*. Randon House, A Stepping Stone Book, 1987.

_____ *The Stories Julian Tells*. Knopf, 1989.

_____ *Julian, Dream Doctor*. Random House, A Stepping Stone Book, 1990

Coerr, Eleanor *Sadako and the Thousand Paper Cranes*. Yearling Books, 1977.

Coombs, Patricia. *Dorrie and the Haunted House*. (and other titles). Dell, 1980.

Courtney, Vincent. *Virtual Fred*. Random House, A Stepping Stone Book, 1996.

Cresswell, Helen. *Dragon Ride*. Penguin, 1987.

Dahl, Roald. *The Magic Finger*. Penguin, 1974. (Harper & Row, 1966.)

_____ *Roald Dahl's Revolting Rhymes*. Penguin, 1984. (Bantam, 1986.)

_____ *The Fantastic Mr. Fox*. Penguin, 1988. (Bantam, 1978.)

Danziger, Paula. *Amber Brown is not a Crayon*. Scholastic, 1994.

_____ *You Can't Eat Your Chicken Pox Amber Brown*. Scholastic, 1995.

_____ *Amber Brown Wants Extra Credit*. Scholastic, 1996.

Erickson, Russell. *Warton and Morton*. Dell, 1977.

Flor Ada, Alma. *My Name is Maria Isabel*. Aladdin, 1993.

Fox, Paula. *Maurice's Room*. Macmillan, 1988.

Gannett, Ruth Stiles. *The Dragons of Blueland*. Knopf, 1963.

_____ *My Father's Dragon*. Random House, 1948.

_____ *Elmer and the Dragon*. Knopf, 1987.

Gavin, Jamila. *Grandpa Chatterji*. Mammoth, 1994.

Hayes, Geoffrey. *Graveyard Creeper Mystery # 2 House of the Horrible Ghosts*. Random House, 1997.

Heide, Florence Parry. *The Shrinking of Treehorn*. Penguin, 1971. (Holiday, 1971. Dell, 1979.)

Hughes, Shirley. *It's Too Frightening For Me*. Penguin, 1986.

_____ *Chips and Jessie*. Fontana Young Lions, 1985.(Lothrop, 1986.)

Hughes, Ted. *The Iron Man*. Faber and Faber, 1986.

_____ The Iron Woman. Faber, 1995

Hutchins, Pat. *The House That Sailed Away*. Fontana, 1975.

Kinsey-Warnock, Natalie. *The Canada Geese Quilt*. Yearling, 1989.

Kline, Suzy. *Horrible Harry in Room 2B*. (and other titles). Puffin Books, 1997.

Kurtz, Jane. *Fire on the Mountain*. Aladdin, 1998.

Laurin, Anne. *Perfect Crane*. Harper & Row, 1987.)

Le Guin, Ursula K. *Catwings*. Scholastic Inc. 1988.

MacLachlan, Patricia. *Sarah Plain and Tall*. Harper & Row, 1985.

_____ *Seven Kisses in a Row*. 1988.

_____ *Journey*. Delacorte Press, 1991.

_____ *Skylark*. Harper Trophy, 1994.

Martin, Rafe. *The Boy Who Lived With The Seals*. Paper Star, 1996.

McMullan, K.H. *Dragon Slayers' Acadamy*. (series).

_____ *The New Kid At School. - Revenge of Dragon Lady*. Grosset & Dunlap, 1997.

Moorer, Eva. *Buddy, The First Seeing Eye Dog*. Scholastic, 1996.

Polacco, Patricia. *Mrs. Katz and Tush*. Picture Yearling, 1994.

Rayner, Mary. *Mrs. Pig Gets Cross and Other Stories*. Collins, 1986.

Reid Banks, Lynne. *Harry the Poisonous Centipede*. Collins Red Story-book, 1996.

Rosen, Michael. *Hairy Tales and Nursery Crimes*. Fontana Young Lions, 1987.

Scieszka, Jon. *Time Warp Trio Series: Knights of the Kitchen Table; The Not So Jolly Roger; The Good, The Bad and the Goofy*. Penguin, 1991.

Shrub, Elizabeth. *The White Stallion*. Bantam, 1984.

Smucker, Barbara. *Jacob's Little Giant*. Penguin, 1987.

Yeoman, John. *The Boy Who Sprouted Antlers*. Fontana Young Lions, 1987.

Whelan, Gloria. *Next Spring an Oriole*. Random House, 1987.

_____ *Silver*. Random House, 1994.

White, E.B. *Stuart Little*. Harper & Row, 1945.

_____ *Charlotte's Web*. Harper & Row, 1952.

Williams, Margery. *The Velveteen Rabbit*. Avon Books, 1982.

Wyeth, Sharon Dennis. *Ginger Brown: The Nobody Boy*. Random House,1997.


## Poetry, Nursery Rhymes and Multi Cultural Chants

Agard, John. *I Din Do Nuttin and Other Poems*. Magnet, 1984.

Augarde, Steve. *The Hokey Pokey and Other Party Rhymes. - The Itsy Bitsy Spider and Other Hand Rhymes*. Scholastic, 1996.

Bennett, Jill and Oxenbury, Helen. *Teeny Tiny*. Putnam, 1986.

Boardman, Bob and Diana. *Red Hot Peppers: The Skookum Jump Rope Book of Games, Rhymes and Fancy Footwork. Sasquatch Books, 1993*

Booth, David. *Doctor Knickerbocker and Other Rhymes*. Kids Can Press, 1993.

Briggs, Raymond. *Fee Fi Fo Fum*. Penguin, 1969.

_____ *The Mother Goose Treasury*. Penguin, 1973. (Dell, 1986.)

Brown, Marc. *Play Rhymes*. Puffin, 1987.

_____ *Hand Rhymes*. Puffin, 1985.

Cole, Joanna. *Anna Banana 101 Jump -Rope Rhymes*. A Beech Tree Paperback Book, 1989.

_____ *Pat-a-Cake and Other Play Rhymes*. Mulberry Books, 1992.

Collins, Heather. *One, Two, Buckle My Shoe*. Kids Can Press, 1997.

Cousins, Lucy. *The Little Dog Laughed and other Nursery Rhymes*. *Picturemac, Macmillan*, 1989.

Downie, Mary Alice and Robertson, Barbara (eds.). Illus. By Elizabeth Cleaver. *The New Wind has Wings*. Oxford University Press, 1987.

Dunn, Sonja and Thurman, Mark. *Crackers and Crumbs*. Pembroke Publishers, 1990.

_____ *Give Me a Break Rattlesnake*. Stodddart, 1994.

Fitch, Sheree and Kovalski, Maryann . *Mabel Murple*. Doubleday, 1995.

Greenfield, Eloise. *Honey, I Love and Other Love Poems*. Harper & Row, 1986.

Hallworth, Grace and Binch, Caroline. *Down The River. Afro-Caribbean Rhymes, Games and Songs for Children*. Scholastic, 1996.

Heidbreder, Robert and Karen Patkau. *Don't Eat Spiders*. Oxford University Press, 1987.

_____ *Eenie Meenie Manitoba: Playful Poems and Rollicking Rhymes*. Kids Can Press, 1996.

King, Karen. *Oranges and Lemons*. Oxford University Press, 1987.

Kovalski, Maryann. *The Wheels on the Bus*. Kids Can Press, 1988.

Langford, Mary D. *Hopscotch Around the World*. Morrow Junior Books, 1992

Lee, Dennis. *Garbage Delight*. Macmillan, 1977.

_____ *Alligator Pie*. Macmillan, 1981,

_____ *Jelly Belly*. Macmillan, 1983. (Bedrick Books, 1985.)

Lobel, Arnold. *The Random House Book of Mother Goose*. Random House, 1986.

Lobel, Arnold and Prelutsky, Jack. *The Random House Book of Poetry for Children*. Random House, 1983.

Nikola, Lisa W. *Bein' With You This Way*. Lew & Low Books Inc. 1994.

Prelutsky, Jack. *The New Kid on the Block*. Greenwillow, 1984.

_____ *Read Aloud Rhymes for the Very Young.* Knopf, 1986.

_____ *Ride a Purple Pelican.* Greenwillow, 1986.

_____ *Tyrannosaurus Was A Beast.*, Greenwillow, 1988.

Raffi. *One Light One Sun.* Crown, 1987.

Reid, Barbara. *Sing a Song of Mother Goose.* Scholastic, Inc., 1989.

Rosen, Michael. *You Can't Catch Me.* Penguin, 1983.

_____ *Don't Put Mustard in the Custard.*

_____ *When Did You Last Wash Your Feet?* Andre Deutsch, 1986.

Sendak, Maurice. *We Are All in the Dumps with Jack and Guy.* Harper Collins , 1993.

Silverstein, Shel. *Where the Sidewalk Ends.* Harper & Row, 1975.

_____ *A Light in the Attic.* Harper & Row, 1981.

Smith, Wendy. *Action Songs.* Picture Lions, 1995.

Stones, Rosemary and Mann, Andrew. *Mother Goose Comes to Cable Street.* Penguin, 1980.

Vosar, David. *Yo, Hungry Wolf! A Nursery Rap.* Picture Yearling, 1993.

Watson, Clyde. *Catch Me and Kiss Me and Say It Again.* Collins, 1978. (Putnam, 1983.)

_____ *Father Fox's Pennyrhymes.* Harper & Row, 1987. (Scholastic, Inc., 1975.)

Williams, Sarah. *Round and Round the Garden: Fingerplay Rhymes for the Very Young.* Oxford University Press, 1983.

# SERIES OF BOOKS PUBLISHED FOR YOUNG READERS PRODUCED BY EDUCATIONAL PUBLISHERS

These programs are accompanied by a range of other resources to support their use, such as blackline masters, teachers guides, cassette tapes, and big books. Check out what each one offers by calling your local representative, or viewing these programs at conferences and in-service opportunities.

*Bookshop*    Scholastic Education/Mondo Publishing
High quality books with a variety of sizes, shapes genres, and formats, both fiction and nonfiction, arranged in three stages for Grades K–1, 1–2, and 2–3. Each title comes in sets of six copies. Big books, cassettes, blackline masters, and teacher's guide are also available. Easily blended into a levelled collection of books.

*Early Success*    ITP Nelson/Houghton Mifflin
For Grades 1–2 this program has 30 titles at level 1 and 30 titles at level 2. The titles come in packs of seven making them handy for group work. The books start very easy and gradually increase in difficulty. Teacher's guide, etc. are available.

*First Links*    The Wright Group
This program for kindergarten and Grade 1 classrooms features 112 student books grouped into eight modules: Literature; Letters; Chants; Facts; Words; Rhymes; Concepts; and Readers.

*Foundations*    The Wright Group
Structured to provide material for students who have problems learning to read, this program consists of 237 fiction and nonfiction student books levelled in a finely graded progression from early emergent through early fluency.

*Oxford Reading Tree*
A series of stories which focus on child-centred situations and experiences. Vocabulary and sentence structures are carefully controlled

and key words are repeated throughout the story books, though the emphasis is on natural sounding language. The program is divided into fourteen levels.

*Factfinders* are nonfiction books from the Oxford Reading Tree. They are arranged to correspond to levels 2–9. These books introduce children to the skills they need in order to read and understand information books.

*Meadow Books*   Harcourt Brace
A collection of fine literature for Grades 1–3 arranged in small anthologies as well as single titles. The variety and quality of the stories are excellent. The series is not finely graded.

*PM Library*   Scholastic/Rigby
This program includes story books, alphabet books, read-alongs, fiction, and nonfiction and very easy to read starter books for emergent readers, finely graded and with good consistency of format to help beginning readers.

*Rigby*
Books for individual reading in a variety of genres.

*Sunshine Books*   The Wright Group
Hundreds of little books on a wide variety of topics close to the child's world. This program is comprehensive but not finely graded.

*Twig Books*   The Wright Group
These emergent level books feature nonfiction topics. There are 96 pupil books, 8 read-togethers, and 12 big books

*Wonder World*   The Wright Group
Over 200 fiction and nonfiction student books for Grades K–3, levelled into developmentally appropriate sets from emergent through to fluent literacy.

# REFERENCES

Note:    All children's books cited are found in the bibliography.

*Introduction*

Charlotte Huck, *Literature as the Content of Reading, Theory Into Practice,* The Ohio State University: Vol. 26, Dec. 1987, p. 375.

*Chapter One*

Margaret Meek, *Learning to Read* , London: The Bodley Head, 1982, p. 9.

Frank Smith, *Reading Without Nonesense,* New York: Teachers College Press, 1985, p. 123.

Kenneth Goodman, "Reading: a psycholinguistic guessing game." *Journal of the Reading Specialist,* Vol. 6, 1967. p. 26-35.

Constance Weaver, *Reading Process and Practice: from socio-linguistics to whole language,* Portsmouth, NH: Heinemann Educational Books, 1988.

Michele Landsberg, *Michele Landsberg's Guide to Children's Books,* Markham, Ontario: Penguin Books, 1986, p. 194.

Paul Hazard, *Books, Children and Men.* Boston: The Horn Book, 1944, p. 4.

*Chapter Two*

Lewis, C.S. "The Reader and all kinds of stories," in *The Cool Web: The Pattern of Children's Reading,* Margaret Meek, et al, eds. London, The Bodley Head, 1977, p. 85.

Varley, Susan. *Badger's Parting Gifts.* Translated by My Teng. Magi, 1997,

Yee, Paul. *The Ghost Train.* A Groundwood Book, 1996.

*Chapter Three*

Adams, Marilyn Jager. (1990) *Beginning to Read: Thinking and Learning about Print.* Urbana-Champaign, IL: Center for the Study of Reading, University of Illinois.

*Chapter Four*

Clay, Marie. *An Observation Survey of Early Literacy Achievement.* Portsmouth NH: Heinemann. 1993 a.

*Chapter Six*

Meek, Margaret. *How Texts Teach What Reader's Learn.* Stroud, Gloucester: The Thimble Press, 1988.

# ACKNOWLEDGMENTS

Many fellow educators have helped us to shape our practice, and we thank all those working in the field of children's literature and reading for their contributions to our thinking. In particular, Bob Barton and David Booth have been consistent supporters and friends. Judy Sarick's The Children's Bookstore in Toronto is still one of the best places in Canada to find children's books, and we thank her for letting us browse and read.

We gratefully thank the following people who have helped us work on this book. Dr. Judith Scott provided insight and guidance. Sheila Koffman at Another Story Bookstore has been generous with ideas and advice. Krista Villiers, Gwen Bartnik, and Brenda Boylan are expert literacy teachers who have shared ideas and made suggestions. Maxine Bone gave generously of her time in discussing ideas about guided reading. Library Technician, Luba Andrews, kindly sought bibliographical information. As always, we have had the good fortune to have the encouragement and support of our partners, Jerry George and Charlie Hewins. Thanks to you all.

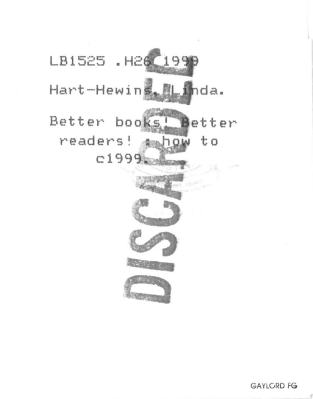

GAYLORD FG